AMERICA'S
NATIONAL PARKS

PUBLICATIONS INTERNATIONAL, LTD.

Contributing Author:

John Boslough is a science writer whose articles have appeared in such publications as *National Geographic, Smithsonian, Psychology Today,* and *Reader's Digest.* He has been the science editor for *U.S. News & World Report.* His recent book about mathematician Stephen Hawking is attracting international attention.

Consultant:

Richard Tourangeau works in the public affairs section of the National Park Service and writes a monthly column for the park service newsletter. During the last 15 years, he has visited 35 national parks.

ISBN 0-88176-959-2
Library of Congress Catalog Card Number: 90-63311

Table of Contents

NATIONAL PARK SYSTEM MAP

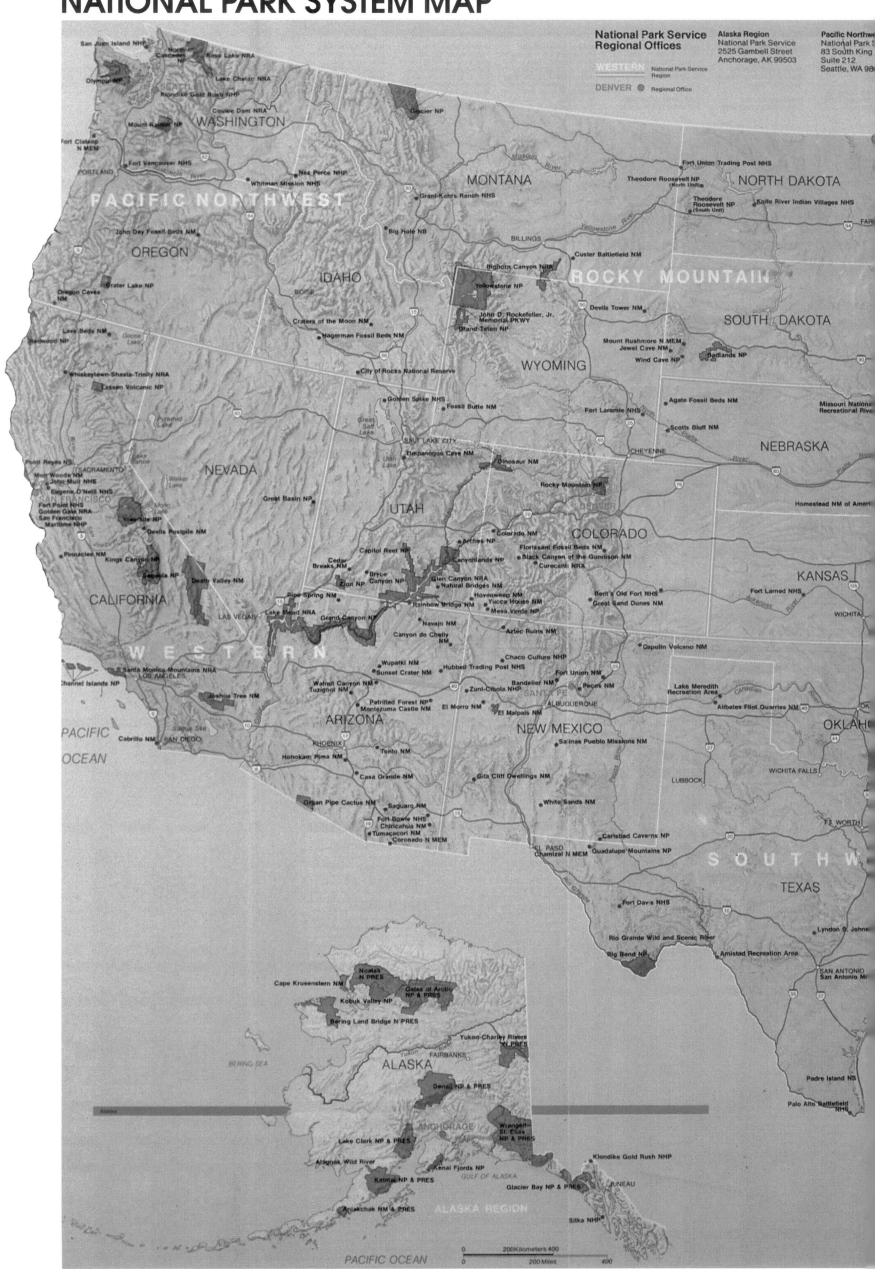

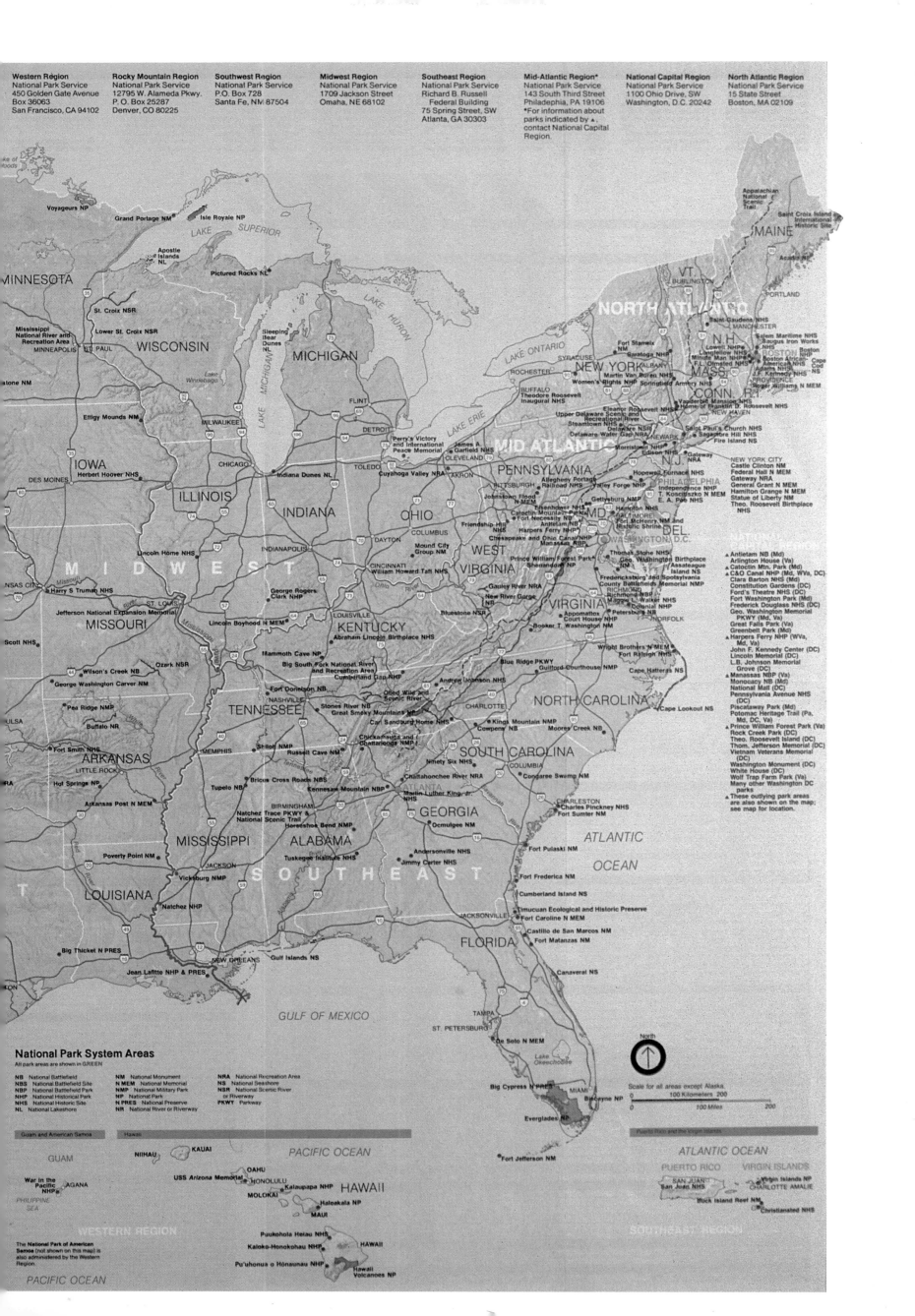

Western Region
National Park Service
450 Golden Gate Avenue
Box 36063
San Francisco, CA 94102

Rocky Mountain Region
National Park Service
12795 W. Alameda Pkwy.
P. O. Box 25287
Denver, CO 80225

Southwest Region
National Park Service
P.O. Box 728
Santa Fe, NM 87504

Midwest Region
National Park Service
1709 Jackson Street
Omaha, NE 68102

Southeast Region
National Park Service
Richard B. Russell
Federal Building
75 Spring Street, SW
Atlanta, GA 30303

Mid-Atlantic Region*
National Park Service
143 South Third Street
Philadelphia, PA 19106
*For information about
parks indicated by ▲
contact National Capital
Region.

National Capital Region
National Park Service
1100 Ohio Drive, SW
Washington, D.C. 20242

North Atlantic Region
National Park Service
15 State Street
Boston, MA 02109

National Park System Areas

All park areas are shown in GREEN

NB National Battlefield	**NM** National Monument	**NRA** National Recreation Area
NBS National Battlefield Site	**N MEM** National Memorial	**NS** National Seashore
NBP National Battlefield Park	**NMP** National Military Park	**NSR** National Scenic River
NHP National Historical Park	**NP** National Park	or Riverway
NHS National Historic Site	**N PRES** National Preserve	**PKWY** Parkway
NL National Lakeshore	**NR** National River or Riverway	

The **National Park of American Samoa** (not shown on this map) is also administered by the Western Region.

The National Park Service
75 Years of Preserving America

Our national parks are as diverse and extraordinary as the land and people that make up our nation. With each passing year as we better understand the impact we are having on our environment, we become more aware of the value of this important national resource. Our national parks preserve America's best wild and wonderful places and also make them available for us to enjoy. In recognition of the seventy-fifth anniversary of the establishment of the National Park Service, this book visits America's 49 national parks from the best-known and best-loved parks—Yellowstone, Great Smoky Mountains, and Yosemite—to the newest and visually dramatic parks in Alaska and American Samoa.

The establishment of Yellowstone as the first national park on March 1, 1872, marked the beginning of a brand-new attitude toward wilderness. Until that time, most Americans had thought of the nation's virgin forests, vast expanses of prairie, pristine waterways, incredibly rich mineral deposits, and other natural assets as sources of personal wealth to be used in whatever way any individual who owned them or happened to find them wanted. But the astonishing natural wonders of Yellowstone were a catalyst that began to change the predominate American attitude about wilderness from a desire to exploit into a wish to protect.

In the late 1860s, rumors began circulating in Washington, D.C., about an otherworldly land of bizarre topography, bubbling hot springs, geysers erupting a hundred feet in the air, and other phenomenal thermal spectacles in the Yellowstone region of the Rocky Mountains. Three men from Montana, David Folsom, Charles Cook, and William Peterson, were dispatched to the area in 1869 to prove or puncture the rumors. Their reports left many people as skeptical as ever, so the following year a survey team under the leadership of the Surveyor General of Montana, Henry Washburn, systematically explored Yellowstone and reported back that even the most fantastic rumors about the place were pretty close to being absolutely true. Keeping careful records as they moved through the region, the 19 explorers named the thermal wonders, usually picking epithets derived from the netherworld.

By law the explorers were entitled to stake individual claims on the territory and its natural wonders. But one evening, at the junction of the Firehole, Gibbon, and Madison rivers, the men sat around what has proved to be one of history's most significant campfires. They had been talking about the way in which they were planning to divide Yellowstone among themselves, when one member of the expedition, a young attorney named Cornelius Hedges, eloquently proposed another alternative: Instead of seeking private gain, the men should persuade the federal government to preserve the Yellowstone region in its entirety. All but one member of the party agreed. When the men returned home, they lobbied vigorously for government protection of the area. They were highly persuasive, and in March 1872 Congress passed legislation creating the world's first—and what many believed would be the only—national park "as a pleasuring ground for the benefit and enjoyment of the people."

By the turn of the century, Sequoia, Yosemite, and Mount Rainier had been established. John Muir, who adored the Yosemite Valley and the Sierra Nevada, campaigned energetically for a park in that area. Concerned that sheep were overgrazing the region and that advancing civilization threatened the giant sequoias, Muir elicited the help of Robert Underwood Johnson, an editor of *The Century*, which at that time was one of the country's most widely read magazines. Johnson published two passionately written articles by Muir in the magazine, quickly making Yosemite into a national issue. Public opinion encouraged Congress to establish Yosemite National Park in 1890. At the same time, Sequoia and General Grant, which is now part of Kings Canyon, were mandated. John Muir also played a significant role in the establishment of Mount Rainier, Grand Canyon, and Petrified Forest national parks.

During his presidency Theodore Roosevelt put forth his best efforts on behalf of the fledgling national park system. After spending four days in Yosemite with Muir, Roosevelt became convinced that the park should be expanded to include the spectacular Yosemite Valley, and by the end of his term in office, this area was also protected. During Roosevelt's presidency, Crater Lake, Mesa Verde, and Wind Cave national parks were established, and land that is now part of Grand Canyon, Lassen Volcanic, and Petrified Forest was set aside.

By 1916 there were 11 national parks and 18 national monuments covering more than four and a half million acres of land in the western part of the United States. Cavalry units patrolled much of the parkland and engineers from the U.S. Army managed the rest. Many people involved with administering the parks and monuments became aware that a single agency ought to be running the entire park system. In 1916 Congress passed legislation establishing the National Park Service within the Department of the Interior. The new agency, headed by Steve Mather, took on a dual assignment to preserve the territory lying within park boundaries in an undisturbed, natural state and also to make the parks available to everyone who wanted to visit them.

There are many different ways to interpret this mandate, and during the last 75 years, the park service has constantly rede-

fined its goals. Congress used to establish a national park to protect something specific: a geyser here, a jagged mountain or unusual forest there. This practice encouraged park administrators and the public to ignore or even damage other areas of the park. As recently as the 1930s, predatory animals were killed to protect visitors and other wildlife, and commercial fishing was allowed in the parks. In Yosemite, for example, woodpeckers have been shot because their rapping upset sleeping lodge guests.

Since the early 1930s, the scope of the National Park Service has broadened. In addition to parks and monuments, Congress has set aside national parkways, seashores, wild and scenic rivers, recreational areas, scenic trails, and other preserves. All these wilderness and recreational areas are under the jurisdiction of the park service. Congress has also created national parks to protect ecologically delicate areas, such as Everglades, Biscayne, and the new national parks in Alaska. The evolving national interest in ecology has changed the way in which the parks are administered. Today the National Park Service works to preserve each park as a whole because each one is a unique statement of this nation's spectacular natural heritage.

The National Park Service now faces challenges that could never have been imagined 75 years ago. Millions of people visit the parks each year, and over the years their expectations about what they will find there have changed radically. Before the 1920s getting to the parks required arduous travel by train and wagon. But automobiles made the parks easily accessible for many Americans. In the 1930s most visitors just wanted to speed by a park's major sights for a quick look and then to be entertained by animal acts, drive-though sequoia trees, sound-and-light shows, and other amusements that were only marginally related to their wilderness setting. In the 1950s many visitors made one national park the destination for their entire vacation. Family car campers overfilled park campground, bringing with them all the comforts of home, including portable radios, charcoal cookers, and mountains of throw-away packaging material. Beginning in the 1970s the park service started to make difficult but necessary choices that are returning the national parks to their original mandate. Use of the parks is being limited to activities that appreciate the natural wonder of the parklands. Natural cycles are reestablishing themselves; food chains are rebuilding. Animals that had almost completely disappeared, including buffalo, wolves, white trumpeter swans, and prairie dogs, have been successfully reintroduced.

There is much that still needs to be accomplished to preserve the wilderness and to meet the additional challenge of making it accessible to everyone who seeks a respite from urban America. In our national parks, there is almost no logging, no hunting, no mining, and no grazing. Trees are left where they fall; forests are allowed to heal themselves following the devastation of fire or volcanic eruption. Our national parks are the definitive statement of traditional American idealism. The great wealth of this nation has always been our natural resources. The careful preserving of large tracts of wilderness expresses our respect for ourselves and our hope for the future. America's national parks preserve more than stunningly beautiful scenery; they give each of us the right to feel proud that we as a nation have set aside part of our incredible land to remain wild and untamed by civilization. Even if you never visit the parks, just knowing that they are there should give you a strong sense of national pride.

Let *America's National Parks* take you on a photographic journey across the continental United States, starting in the nation's first park, Yellowstone. From there you travel to Acadia, an island off the rocky coast of Maine; forested Isle Royale in Lake Superior; and Virgin Islands, a Caribbean paradise of white sand, sparkling water, and stunningly beautiful coral reefs. Then you move north up the eastern half of the United States from the vast swamplands of Everglades to the waterways of Voyageurs stopping to visit mountains, caves, and hot springs. Moving west your armchair journey takes you through a phenomenal variety of fascinating landscapes from the rugged Badlands of North and South Dakota to the desert canyons of Big Bend in Texas. Throughout this arid terrain, water has sculpted the land into meandering canyons, deep gorges, high tablelands, spires, and freestanding arches. Grand Canyon opens the earth's surface to reveal the incredible beauty of its geology, while Petrified Forest, Bryce Canyon, Zion, Canyonlands, and Arches exhibit the complexity of rock sculpted by nature.

After crossing the Continental Divide in Rocky Mountain, you travel through Great Basin, a new park with sweeping vistas and high mountains. The Sierra Nevada wilderness in Redwood, Yosemite, Sequoia, and Kings Canyon offers visitors the solitude of rugged hiking trails along with some of the best-known sights in the national parks, including Yosemite Valley and the giant sequoias. In the parks located in the Cascades, volcanoes have been the major earth-shaping force: some now sleep under glaciers, crater lakes, or rain forests; others still smolder.

Out in the Pacific, four island parks offer visitors very different experiences. Channel Islands protects kelp beds and sea life just off the coast of southern California. Haleakala is an enormous dormant volcano with a desert in its crater and tropical rain forests climbing its eastern slope. Active volcanoes regularly erupt in the park on Hawaii, sending bright flares of orange lava high into the sky. America's newest park, American Samoa, is a tropical wonderland with pristine beaches, coral reefs busy with sea life, and dense rain forests. In sharp contrast to the lushness of this island paradise, your tour of the national parks concludes with visits to the eight spectacular parks in Alaska. From the thunderous splash of a glacier breaking into pale blue icebergs at Glacier Bay to awesome views of magnificent Denali (Mount McKinley), North America's tallest mountain, Alaska's parks preserve and protect some of the planet's most spectacular wilderness.

From swampy wetlands to treeless mountaintops, from seacoasts to deserts, the scenery in America's national parks is a breathtaking array of contrasting images. The dynamic full-color photographs of *America's National Parks* encompass the rich diversity and scenic beauty of the parks, presenting America at its most beautiful. Throughout this anniversary year and for many years to come, you and your family will enjoy this tribute to our magnificent national parks.

Yellowstone
Thermal Wonderland

. . . .

Splashing down from a height of 308 feet, the Lower Falls propels the river though Yellowstone's Grand Canyon between rugged walls of volcanic rock dyed brilliant yellow by minerals in the water.

Opposite: *Mighty Old Faithful regularly sends majestic columns of water shooting as high as 200 feet into the bright blue Wyoming sky.*

Right: *The silvery orb of the moon adds its radiance to the glimmering planes and pools of Minerva Terrace at Mammoth Hot Springs near the park's north entrance.*

The volcanic cauldron beneath Yellowstone creates enormous plumes of water belching out of the earth from steaming vents. More than half of the world's geysers are located within the park, and Yellowstone is also blessed with a proliferation of hot springs, fumaroles, and teaming pools of evanescent colors and algae. Here you will find percolating streams, bubbling creeks, and gushing rivers, and almost everywhere in the park, you encounter the acrid and unmistakable smell of sulfur.

In 1872, when Yellowstone was made the world's first national park, Wyoming was not yet a state, and the United States was still a pioneer nation. Its western frontiers overflowed with splendid scenery and a profusion of wild animals. The first visitors to the park certainly did not come to see wilderness. Yellowstone was attractive to its first visitors because of its extraordinary wealth of geysers and fumaroles. These hearty adventurers made the arduous trek to the remote park by wagon. In the intervening century, civilization moved west, and the frontier, including most of the animals, disappeared. The thermal extravaganza is still as spectacular as ever. But today's visitors to Yellowstone also appreciate the park as a sanctuary for wildlife and a preserve of pristine wilderness.

Yellowstone's boundaries encompass some of America's most spectacular untouched wilderness: jagged peaks, endless forests, rugged canyons, crystal-clear lakes, and alpine meadows. Roaming this terrain is an array of western wildlife unmatched elsewhere: buffalo, elk, deer, grizzly bear, black bear, osprey, eagle, coyote, cougar, beaver, white pelican, and moose. More than two million acres of Rocky Mountain wilder-

. . . .

At Mammoth Hot Springs superheated water rises to the surface through limestone rather than lava, creating terraces of smooth travertine.

• •

ness provide a safe and vast habitat for all this wildlife. Ninety-nine percent of the parkland is undeveloped.

Nature runs by its own time schedule in Yellowstone. This is a place to sit still and let the magic of nature amaze you. You may catch the colors of a rainbow through a plummeting waterfall. Hike along a marsh, and in time you might see a bull moose stride out of the forest and wade through ankle-deep water. Or you may see a family of black bears romping and wrestling in a meadow beside a mountain stream. Keep your eyes on the high branches of a lodgepole pine long enough, and eventually the head of a bald eagle may emerge from the thicket of its nest.

Stand quietly on a bank of the Yellowstone River; a merganser paddles along enjoying the day. Upstream a native cutthroat leaps out of the water to see what the duck is doing, but the fish is oblivious to the danger of the great osprey circling 200 feet overhead. Watch closely because the bird is incredibly swift when it dives for its prey. Early in the morning during the autumn, you may hear the eerie bugling of a bull elk, but then again you may not, because this place doesn't run on an established sched-

ule. Even the park's thermal attractions operate on their own secret timetables: Old Faithful erupts every 50 to 80 minutes, not on the hour as many of us learned in school.

An enduring myth about Yellowstone holds that Native Americans stayed away from the area because of its strange and frightening thermal features. In fact, people have lived here since the retreat of the most recent ice age nearly 9,000 years ago. In 1807 a Native American probably told trapper John Colter about a place where hot water and steam issue from the earth. This member of the Lewis and Clark expedition is credited with the discovery of Yellowstone. Then as now it was obvious that this is an extraordinary place where something highly unusual is going on beneath the surface of the earth to generate enough heat to create this garden of thermal wonders. Geologists have discovered that the earth's crust is extraordinarily thin in the Yellowstone region. In most places on the planet, the crust is about 20 miles thick and floats on a mantle that consists of molten rock, or magma. In Yellowstone the earth's crust is only about two miles thick. The seething hot mantle heats the ground above it, which in turn heats the water in the springs and geysers.

Morning Glory Pool in Upper Geyser Basin brings to the surface a glorious spectrum of color from deep within the earth.

Celebrated in anecdote, cartoon, and caricature, Yellowstone is the park most people probably think of when they think of a national park. It is also a study of the way in which a park should be run, but this was not always the case. During Yellowstone's first decade as a national park, geysers were vandalized; game, particularly bison, was slaughtered by park officials and sportsmen; and politicians gave away its land as concessions to supporters. In 1886 the U.S. Army took over administration of the park and built roads and the park headquarters near the north boundary. The park became a model of efficiency, which operators of other parks in the fledgling park system attempted to imitate. Beginning in 1916, when it was established, the National Park Service has run the park with dedication and skill.

Undine Falls continues its steady downward course even after winter snows have enchanted the forest with their still, soft whiteness.

Opposite: *Lake Yellowstone spreads out over more than 100 square miles at the base of the Absarokas, the rugged range of mountains that defines the eastern boundary of Yellowstone.*

The water that flows out of Grand Prismatic Spring was heated in the molten interior of our planet, which is closer to the surface at Yellowstone than it is anywhere else on earth.

Geysers and Fumaroles

Geysers, springs of hot bubbling water, or fumaroles issuing sulfurous steam seem to occur almost everywhere you turn in Yellowstone. Elsewhere there are mud pots and underground explosions, or the earth is hot to the touch. Obviously something spectacular is going on just below the surface. To understand the thermal wonders in Yellowstone today, we need to go back 75 million years to a time when sections of the earth's crust collided and raised the Rocky Mountains to far greater heights than we now see. About 25 million years later, volcanic activity created still more mountain ranges in the Yellowstone region.

The grand finale of this geological activity occurred about 600,000 years ago when an area within the boundaries of the park suddenly exploded as two giant magma chambers moved to within a few thousand feet of the earth's surface. The landscape was devastated, and volcanic ash and dust spread over thousands of square miles. At the center only a smoldering caldera remained; this enormous, collapsed crater covered an area that was 47 by 27 miles. Geologists believe that Yellowstone's boiling hot springs, mud holes, and geysers are reminders that more violent geological activity is about to happen again.

MONTANA

• Butte   • Billings

Yellowstone

IDAHO   WYOMING

Pocatello •

Cheyenne •

Yellowstone National Park

Established:	1872
Location:	Wyoming, Montana, and Idaho
When to go:	Open all year. (Winter access is limited.)
Size:	2,221,766 acres
Terrain:	Mountains, canyons, lakes, geysers, and hot springs
Interesting sights:	Old Faithful Geyser and Yellowstone River
Wildlife:	Elk, grizzly bear, black bear, deer, moose, eagle, osprey, beaver, mountain lion, and trumpeter swan
Activities:	Ranger-led walks, talks, and campfire programs; hiking, camping, fishing, boating, horseback riding, photography courses, bicycling, stagecoach rides, cross-country skiing, snowshoeing, snowmobiling, snow-coach tours, and backpacking
Services:	Four visitor centers, eight lodges and cabins, and 13 campgrounds
Information:	P.O. Box 168, Yellowstone National Park, Wyoming 82190; 307-344-7381

Geologists believe that Castle Geyser is the park's oldest geyser. Minerals from the hot water and steam of its regular eruptions have built a cone around the geyser that is 120 feet high and still growing.

Acadia
Islands Primeval

· · · · · · · · · · · · · · · · · · · ·

The ocean relentlessly pounds the east coast of Mount Desert Island, wearing away everything but the island's hard granite core.

Opposite: *The soft light of an autumn morning breaks through sea fog to reveal rocks smoothed by glaciers and fall's bright colors on Cadillac Mountain.*

Right: *Scraped out by glaciers, the many large and small lakes of Mount Desert Island provide an ideal habitat for the large beaver population, which in earlier times attracted French and English fur traders to the island.*

Acadia National Park is a nearly perfect summation of Maine's spectacular coast; it is at once dramatic and sublime. Completely surrounded by the sea, the park's glacier-scoured interior consists of lovely valleys, lakes, and peaks. As they have for centuries, wave and wind sculpt its rugged coast. Cadillac Mountain, which is 1,530 feet high, is one of the places where dawn first brushes the United States. Daylight greets this mountaintop in spectacular waves of purple, red, and blue. Four miles west a deep coastal valley has been filled by the sea to create Somes Sound, the only true fjord in the southern 48 states. Across an inlet the Schoodic Peninsula is a remote, untamed intrusion into the ocean where enormous granite rocks brace against the endless lashing of the waves.

The park is in a region that was once a French colonial territory called La Cadie. The area was first explored in 1604 by Samuel de Champlain. His ship crashed into a shoal off the coast and required extensive repairs. While Champlain's party was stranded, he led them ashore to explore the interior. There he encountered people from the Abnaki tribe who lived on the island during the summer. Because of its hills, mountains, and rugged coast, they called it Pemetic, "the sloping land." Champlain renamed the pristine island, blessed with forests, lakes, and mountains, L'Isle des Monts Déserts, or "the island of desert mountains," because from the sea it looked barren and wasted. Interested mainly in the island's beavers because their pelts drew high prices in Europe, Champlain returned to France with tales of the wondrous place. A French mission was established there a few years later. Following a century and a half of war between the French and British over control of the New World, the island finally fell into the hands of the English in 1763, just 13 years before the American Revolution.

· · · · · · · · · · · · · · · · · · · ·

During the late-nineteenth and early-twentieth centuries, millionaires, including John D. Rockefeller, began spending their summers on Mount Desert Island. By 1917 Rockefeller became convinced that the rapidly proliferating automobile would soon destroy the island's natural beauty and serenity, so he undertook the construction of an elaborate network of gravel paths. The roadways were for horse-drawn carriages only. Automobiles were not allowed on the 57 miles of paths and 17 granite bridges, each exquisitely built by hand. Later Rockefeller donated the paths, bridges, and 11,000 acres of his land to Acadia National Park. Today the park occupies about half the island as well as several smaller islands. Private estates and charming coastal villages comprise the rest of the land on Mount Desert Island. Rockefeller's carriageways are still in use and still not open to automobiles. Today they provide an easy, civilized, and inviting route into the park for walkers, horseback riders, bicyclists, joggers, and in winter, cross-country skiers.

Action of Glaciers

Acadia National Park owes its dramatic beauty to the action of glaciers during one of the most recent ice ages. About two millennia ago, Mount Desert Island sat atop a steep granite ridge on the edge of the North American continental mainland. When enormous sheets of ice, as much as two or three miles thick, advanced from the north, glaciers flowed over the tops of the coastal mountains. When the great glaciers moved, they smoothed the tops of the mountains, scraping out large pits that later became lakes and gouging out valleys and passes through the mountains.

The glaciers began melting as the earth's atmosphere warmed. The corresponding rise in the level of the oceans flooded many of the coastal valleys, creating inlets and harbors and also cutting off sections of the shoreline from the mainland. A quick glance at the map makes it readily apparent that Mount Desert Island was formed in this way. Its lake-studded, mountainous interior is a testimony to the work of ice 20,000 years ago.

Acadia National Park

Established:	1919
Location:	Maine
Size:	41,408 acres
When to go:	Open all year. (Winter access is limited.)
Terrain:	Mountains, lakes, valleys, rugged coastline, and beaches
Interesting sights:	Cadillac Mountain and Schoodic Peninsula
Wildlife:	Muskrat, beaver, sea gull, herring gull, bald eagle, bullfrog, bottle-nosed dolphin, small mammals, and birds
Activities:	Ranger-led nature walks, films, slide shows, and bus tours; carriage rides, hayrides, hiking, cycling, horseback riding, swimming, fishing, cross-country skiing, snowshoeing, ice fishing, and snowmobiling
Services:	Visitor center, museum, and two campgrounds
Information:	P.O. Box 177, Bar Harbor, Maine 04609; 207-288-3338

MAINE

Bangor •

Augusta •

Portland • ▲ Acadia

During the most recent ice age, a sheet of ice carried this boulder from a ledge at least 20 miles away to the top of Cadillac Mountain, the highest point on the East Coast.

Isle Royale
Island Wilderness

The Feldtmann Ridge Trail follows a ridge that runs along the southern flank of Isle Royale. This high, open ridge is forested with a stunning mix of hardwoods, including sugar maple, yellow birch, and red oak.

Opposite: *Raspberry Island is a tiny spit of granite southeast of the main island. It was once a high ridge, but rising water in Lake Superior filled the valley, creating this and several other small islands along Rock Harbor.*

Right: *Looking out across an expanse of cold and unpredictable Lake Superior, the tall pines of a small island in Isle Royale National Park are silhouetted against the warm glow of the red sun.*

Separated from mainland Michigan by 56 miles of rough water, Isle Royale is pure wilderness, with no roads and almost no development. The island's isolation has helped to keep it a wild, rugged land that today looks much as it did more than two centuries ago when white men first stepped on its shores. This is the only place in the United States south of Alaska where wolves roam free and where they still play a useful role in the local ecology by preying on weaker members of another species. Moose, the wolf's main prey, also inhabit the island. While the wolves are elusive, you frequently see moose in the meadows along-side woodland trails.

The 45-mile-long island rises out of the vastness of Lake Superior, the largest of the Great Lakes. It is the biggest island in any of the lakes. This unusual national park consists of Isle Royale and another 200 smaller islands. Visitors usually reach Isle Royale on a boat operated by the park service. The ride takes two and a half hours. This park is favored by people who enjoy isolated wilderness, and most park visitors.

On Isle Royale you are truly in the forest primeval. A long ridge extends along the length of the island; its landscape has been complicated by aeons of geological upheaval and sculpting by glaciers. Isle Royale was born as glacial ice withdrew during the last Pleistocene ice age 10,000 years ago. The island's high ridges rose above the great basin that eventually would become Lake Superior, and glacier-scoured gouges in the barren rock became the island's lakes. Wind and water forged a lovely coastline punctuated by numerous inlets and quiet little coves. Soon the first migrants, including mosses, lichens, and wind- and bird-borne seeds, arrived and found little nooks and crannies in

which to begin the arduous work of building soil and vegetation.

Animals also found their way to the island, and a unique ecosystem began evolving. Humans probably first came to Isle Royale about 4,500 years ago. There are more than 1,000 small copper mining pits scattered around the island. The pits were dug in about B.C. 2,500. Moose, the island's largest inhabitants, swam from the mainland early in this century. Wolves, the island's most famous residents, crossed the frozen ice of the lake in the 1940s. Since the late 1950s, scientists have used the island's isolated ecosystem as a natural laboratory in which to study the relationship between wolf as predator and moose as prey.

The noble timber wolf once hunted unhindered across the entire Northern Hemisphere, but now Isle Royale is the only place in the southern 48 states where this majestic creature roams free.

. . . .

Isle Royale National Park

Established:	1931
Location:	Michigan
When to go:	June to September. (The park is closed November to mid-April.)
Size:	571,790 acres
Terrain:	Wilderness island, coves, lakes, and valleys
Interesting sight:	Ancient copper mines
Wildlife:	Moose, timber wolf, beaver, squirrels, fox, and birds
Activities:	Ranger-led nature and history walks, canoe tours, and lighthouse and copper mine tours; films, boating, canoeing, hiking, scuba diving, fishing, and backpacking
Services:	Visitor center, one lodge, and backcountry campsites
Information:	87 North Ripley Street, Houghton, Michigan 49931; 906-482-0984

Island Wolves

Perhaps drawn by a large and growing moose herd, a few wolves crossed the frozen water of Lake Superior to Isle Royale in 1949. For two decades the wolves fed on old, young, or weak moose. Both the moose herd and the wolf pack benefited from the relationship. The wolves prevented the moose from overpopulating the island and eating themselves out of house and home. The wolf pack itself leveled out at about 50 members, which was appropriate for the size of the moose herd.

By about 1980 the symbiosis was no longer working. There were fewer moose upon which the wolves could prey, and the wolf population was falling. By 1989 the moose population had again increased, but there were only 11 wolves left. Park biologists are mystified at the continued drop in the number of wolves. One reason for the decline may be that wolves breed slowly: Only the dominant pair of wolves in a pack produces a litter each year.

This 45-mile-long, densely forested island is dotted with 27 named lakes and innumerable beaver ponds and bogs.

Virgin Islands
Caribbean Paradise

A unique national treasure in a beautiful setting, Virgin Islands National Park is one of just two national parks that do not lie within the 50 United States. (The newest national park in American Samoa is the other park located in a U.S. territory.) Trunk Bay on the northern side of St. John is one of the loveliest vistas in the entire Caribbean, a tropical region known for its exceptionally lovely views of lush isles, white beaches, towering mountains, and old pirate strongholds. The view from the bay is a series of impossibly beautiful, palm-ringed beaches and the whitest sand you have ever seen glistening in the sun. Sailboats dance in the sparkling blue water, and off in the distance Whistling Cay, a small speck of land floating in an azure sea, changes color on a whim of the sky. During the nineteenth century, customs officers used the tiny island as a lookout for smugglers sailing between St. John and the nearby British Virgin Islands.

Within the park's borders are about 9,000 acres of spectacular Caribbean beaches, forests, and mountains, as well as 5,650 undersea acres and several stunning underwater nature trails. The park encompasses about three-quarters of St. John, the third largest island in the U.S. Virgin Islands. Here you will find an incredible diversity of plant life, owing to a huge amount of annual rainfall as well as the island's exposure to spore-bearing winds. In the park's interior, as you wander through high-elevation subtropical forests, you can see more than 800 plant species. Down lower you can walk through dry, desertlike areas as well as mangrove swamps that are rich with mangoes, palms, soursops, turpentine trees, and century plants.

The sparkling white beaches of the island invite park visitors to come down to the sea, where beneath the surface of the water they will find an exquisite world of form and color amid an extensive coral reef.

Opposite: *Trunk Bay brings together the intense blue of Caribbean waters with bright white sand, composed of surf-ground coral, and intensely green tropical forests.*

Right: *On St. John the higher you climb, the more dense the tropical vegetation becomes, because the moist trade winds bathe the heights with constant rainfall.*

St. John is one of about 100 jewellike islands that dot the blue waters of the northern Caribbean. The islands were visited by Columbus in 1493. Imagining the array of islands to be more extensive than it is, he named them for the 11,000 virgins who accompanied St. Ursula on her ill-fated pilgrimage to Rome. For the next two centuries, the only Europeans to come to the islands were pirates, but in the seventeenth century, Danish settlers built vast sugar plantations, using slave laborers imported from Africa. The long association of the Virgin Islands with Europe enhances the extraordinary natural beauty of St. John with the old-world architecture of its towns and villages. A tropical climate and cooling trade winds make the island an ideal vacation spot.

The Virgin Islands owe their natural beauty to the fire of volcanoes. Geologists believe eruptions first occurred about 100 million years ago on the floor of the ocean thousands of feet below the surface. Over many aeons molten rock flowed from volcanic vents, forming the foundation of St. John. About 30 million years after the island building began, the seafloor itself began to rise, lifted up by cataclysmic geologic forces. The final phase in the construction of St. John was a series of violent eruptions above the sea that created a large island of solidified lava covered by sedimentary rocks, primarily limestone formed from the remains and secretions of marine plants and animals. It was not long until seeds of plants borne aloft by the trade winds began the spectacular greening of St. John, preparing the island as a welcoming habitat for animals arriving from the mainland. The island's scores of bird species flew in of their own accord, but lizards and other reptiles floated ashore by accident.

U.S. VIRGIN ISLANDS

San Juan

PUERTO RICO

Virgin
Islands

Underwater Nature Trail

One of the most intriguing aspects of Virgin Islands National Park is its spectacular underwater realm. The park contains a stunning marine preserve where visitors can explore the complexity of life beneath the sea. Here are coral reefs, broad expanses of underwater grassland, and white sands moving slowly in the water. This lovely, complex, and extremely fragile community of plants and animals forms an exquisite and dynamic underwater reef ecosystem.

One of the park's nature trails beneath the sea is in lovely Trunk Bay. Special underwater plaques guide snorkelers through the intricacies of one of the coral reefs that ring the island. As you swim along the trail, signs explain how the reef was formed and indicate the kinds of underwater life you are likely to see. In addition to coral, brilliantly colored conchs, black sea urchins, brittle starfish, and a host of other exquisitely colored creatures also inhabit the reefs.

Virgin Islands National Park

Established:	1956
Location:	U.S. Virgin Islands
When to go:	Open all year
Size:	14,689 acres
Terrain:	Volcanic island ringed by beaches and coral reefs
Interesting sight:	Trunk Bay
Wildlife:	Brain coral, star coral, staghorn coral, coral shrimp, moray eel, yellowtail snapper, French grunt, sharknose gobie, sand diver, and hundreds of species of fish, birds and reptiles
Activities:	Ranger-led hikes, snorkel tours, and interpretive talks; self-guided nature and underwater trails; snorkeling, swimming, boating, and fishing
Services:	Two visitor centers, contact center, and one campground
Information:	10 Estate Nazareth, St. Thomas, U.S. Virgin Islands 00802; 809-775-6238

The forests on St. John have been making a slow but steady comeback since the island's sugar and cotton plantations were abandoned in the nineteenth century after slavery was outlawed.

Everglades
Wetland Wonderland

· ·

Alligators look something like their ancestors, the dinosaurs, but these very large reptiles, with very tiny brains that make up only one percent of their total weight, are far from being extinct in Everglades National Park.

Opposite: *The Shark River Slough brings vital water to the Everglades as it flows in very slowly from central Florida north of the park.*

Right: *As the sun sets over the Gulf of Mexico, it silhouettes lacy pine trees growing on a hammock.*

Prehistoric, frightening, wild, and fascinating, the crocodile rules Everglades. When you see one of these great creatures surging through the turgid waters of a mangrove swamp, its tapered snout sprouting enormous fangs and its great knobby back looking like a moving island, fascination almost overcomes your fear. There is no question that these great reptiles are sovereigns of this wetland wonderland. When a crocodile wants its progress unimpeded by other animals, including the few brave people who dare venture into its domain deep within the swamps, it gives the water a loud, angry whack with its tail. Everyone and everything had best scurry for cover.

Everglades is the only place in the United States where crocodiles can still be found. The great, atavistic reptile is an appropriate symbol of Everglades National Park. Like the park, crocodiles are wild, awesome, and unfathomable. This is one of the world's most complex ecosystems in what looks like an endless swamp of still water, saw grass, junglelike hammocks (masses of vegetation that look like islands), mangrove forests, and thick black muck. The park occupies the southern part of the Everglades, a great body of sluggishly moving water that is more than 5,000 square miles in size and extends from Lake Okeechobee and Big Cypress Swamp to the Gulf of Mexico. Limestone rimming the area acts as a natural barrier against the sea. This is a place so alive with plants and animals that you can almost feel the pulse of nature.

Living wonders abound in Everglades: In the air there are butterflies of every color along with bird after bird; on the ground snails and frogs; and in the water colorful fish of countless varieties, along with alligators and crocodiles. The

· ·

mix of plant and animal life in the Everglades is unique on our planet. It is a subtropical wilderness, containing more than 700 plant and 300 bird species, that provides a haven for many endangered species, including the great crocodiles and their smaller cousins, the alligators, along with the egret, bald eagle, Florida panther, and manatee.

Here, in the swamp, there is much to be learned about the unusual adaptations and delicate balances that support the Everglades's stunning array of life. You might see white egg sacs on a branch that will soon hatch apple snails, the main food of the endangered snail kite, which has a special bill for removing the snails from their shells. Or you might learn about a fish called the gar that has a primitive lung, which allows it to live entirely encased in mud during the dry season. The source of all this life is water and its yearly cycle of flow and drought. During the wet season, from mid-April to mid-December, the Everglades becomes a river only inches deep but miles wide. It flows so slowly that its movement is all but invisible. In the dry season, during the winter months, the park's rich pulse of life slows down and awaits the new flow of water. Every kind of life in the park from plankton to panthers depends upon this annual rhythm. Even people function on this natural time-table; park officials schedule most activities during the dry season, since high humidity and clouds of insects, especially mosquitos, make the wet season extremely disagreeable.

Congress created the first national parks, such as Yellow-stone and Yosemite, to preserve spectacular and unusual scenery. Established in 1947, Everglades National Park was the first park specifically designated to protect a large fragile ecosystem that was facing a grave threat from encroaching civilization. Because human activity was interfering with the yearly water cycle, this land was in extreme danger of being destroyed. Water once flowed out of Lake Okeechobee without interference, but the development of southern Florida began to overwhelm the Everglades about a century ago when large tracts of wetland were considered potentially rich for agriculture

A hearty pond apple tree makes a welcome perch for a great egret in this vast expanse of water and grass that stretches out to the horizon and extends for miles and miles.

and drained. Since then more canals, levees, and dikes have diverted more and more vital water from the Everglades to agribusinesses and commercial or residential developments.

In 1939 immense fires spread across the Everglades as the result of overdraining. In the 1960s retaining walls were built on the south shore of Lake Okeechobee, and land has been developed in Big Cypress Swamp. This has disrupted the natural flow of water and poses a serious threat to the park's ecosystem. Today irrigated farmland comes right up to the park's gates. In the past few years, the number of herons in the park has dramatically declined, and there are just a few Florida panthers left out of a population that once roamed southern Florida at will. Park officials want to purchase privately held wetlands east of the park in the hope that this will give Everglades a greater share of the water it so desperately needs. If its area can be extended, the park will be able to continue to protect this extremely fragile and valuable ecosystem.

Slash pines are naturally fireproof. These spindly trees are sheathed in multilayered bark, and in case of fire only the outer layer is burned off.

Orlando

FLORIDA

Miami

Everglades

Exploring Everglades

Despite the fact that this imposing wetland seems to go on forever with only isolated patches of dry land, there are a number of ways to penetrate and explore Everglades. In addition to boats and canoes, the park also has a number of nature trails that lead into the heart of this wilderness. Gumbo-Limbo Trail is one of the quickest ways to explore the rich terrain of the park. This third-of-a-mile-long loop winds through mango trees and ends at a junglelike hammock. The little raised island of tropical hardwood trees includes several stunning strangler figs and seems to float above a spectacular sea of saw grass, inhabited by flocks of herons and egrets.

The hammock's slight elevation above the surrounding water supports a startling array of life, including foxes, raccoons, snakes, deer, and birds. There are also solution holes here. These depressions in the limestone bedrock hold moisture during the dry season and become habitats for many kinds of insects and birds. As these solution holes fill with organic material, such as bird droppings, they become tiny ecosystems and may eventually become hammocks themselves.

Everglades National Park

Established:	1947
Location:	Florida
When to go:	Open all year
Size:	1,400,533 acres
Terrain:	Swampy area, hammocks, and saw grass prairies
Interesting sight:	Gumbo-Limbo Trail
Wildlife:	Alligator, fox, raccoon, deer, birds, fish, Florida panther, crocodile, and insects
Activities:	Ranger-led walks, talks, hikes, and evening programs; tram tours; boat, canoe, houseboat, motorboat, and bicycle rides; fishing, shrimping, and backpacking
Services:	Two visitor centers, information station, ranger station, park lodge, and two campgrounds
Information:	P.O. Box 279, Homestead, Florida 33030; 305-247-6211

The Gumbo-Limbo Trail, which gets its name from a local tree, is one of many nature trails that convey visitors from the main roads into the heart of the Everglades.

Biscayne
Living Coral

· ·

Below the surface of the ocean, Biscayne comes alive with color as silvery porkfish, stylishly highlighted with bright yellow and black, flit over a huge brain coral that measures several feet in diameter.

Opposite: *The coral reef and shallow waters of Biscayne Bay pose a severe threat to unwary ships. Cape Florida Lighthouse on Key Biscayne marks the northern boundary of the bay.*

Right: *The dread pirate Black Caesar used to prey on ships in this deep channel between Elliot and Old Rhodes keys. Buccaneers are long gone from the bay, but the channel is still called Caesar Creek.*

Warmed by the flow of Gulf Stream waters moving up through the sea like an immense river, Biscayne Bay extends eastward from the heavy mangrove forests of southern Florida to a string of low-lying barrier islands and coral reefs that protect it from the ocean. During the seventeenth century, this bay was the hideaway of the notorious pirate captain Black Caesar. He lured his prey with a tricky ruse of pretending to be adrift in an open boat. When passing ships stopped to rescue the pirate, his crew fell on them in ambush.

The pirates are now long gone, and today Biscayne Bay is patrolled by manatee. With its gentle, doleful face, the manatee is an enormous mammal as long as 13 feet and weighing a ton or more. It uses its front flippers to shove its diet of sea grasses and other underwater plants into its mouth. There are only about 1,000 of these great beasts left; all of them roam the waters off Florida. Along with the manatee, the bay contains a remarkably varied spectrum of dazzling fish, fantastically shaped coral, and vast beds of waving turtle grass. The bay is only four to 10 feet deep, making it a breeding ground for more than 200 kinds of marine creatures, including shrimp, spiny lobsters, sponges, and crabs. Looking into the shallow water, you will see the colorful flash of a parrot fish swimming by, the bright glimmer of an angelfish, or the surprisingly graceful movements of an immense sea turtle.

The park encompasses Biscayne Bay between Key Biscayne and Key Largo, the northernmost islands of the Florida keys. It is the only national park that is almost entirely underwater. Only four percent of its area is on dry land; the rest is an ocean wonderland with its most marvelous vistas lying below the

· ·

surface. The surface areas of the park consist of about 50 barrier islands strung across the water like pearls on a string and the magnificent mangrove shoreline that is one the East Coast's major undeveloped coastal areas. The mangroves help stabilize this shoreline by trapping their own fallen leaves in networks of tangled roots. This decaying matter, rich in protein, provides food for the tiny creatures that occupy the bottom of the bay's extensive food chain. The mangroves also attract many species of birds, including peregrine falcons and bald eagles.

Like nearby Everglades National Park, Biscayne Bay was created by Congress under intense pressure from environmentalists who wanted to save the bay from the threat of developers. In the 1960s plans were made to build resorts and subdivisions on the northern keys. To prevent this from happening, Biscayne Bay was made a national monument in 1968. The protected area was expanded to its present size, which encompasses more keys and reefs, when it became a national park in 1980.

Yellow-tailed porkfish and gold-and-silver cottonwicks live in the warm waters of the Gulf Stream, protected by the only living coral reefs in the continental United States.

Orlando
•

FLORIDA

Miami •
▲Biscayne

Coral Reef

The most prominent life-forms in Biscayne National Park are the extensive communities of underwater coral reefs. These are the only living reefs within the continental United States. Coral comes in many forms. As park visitors tour the bay in glass-bottom boats, the floorshow includes giant brain coral and mountainous star coral. Some of these coral reefs are extremely tall, rising hundreds of feet from the seafloor, with branching shapes that reach out in every direction.

Coral reefs are formed over centuries as colonies of tiny polyps secrete an exoskeleton of calcium carbonate, or limestone, then live within the tiny nooks and crannies of the ever-growing formation. The accumulation of this skeletal material, broken and piled up by wave action, eventually produces a huge, rocky mass that can support an astonishing variety of animal and plant life. All the reefs of Biscayne Bay harbor an array of vibrantly colored fish that flit and flow around the gorgeous formations. You will see filefish, porcupine fish, angelfish, and sharks. Not all coral is hard as rock. In Biscayne Bay you will also see soft corals, such as sea fans, rippling in the calm, clear water.

Biscayne National Park

Established:	1980
Location:	Florida
When to go:	Open all year
Size:	173,039 acres
Terrain:	Underwater coral reefs, barrier islands, and coastal areas
Interesting sight:	Star coral reef
Wildlife:	Pelican, coral, manatee, parrot fish, jackknife fish, cottonwick, rock beauty, and many species of tropical fish and birds
Activities:	Ranger-led canoe trips, nature tours, and glass-bottom boat trips; swimming, snorkeling, scuba diving, water-skiing, boating, fishing, hiking, bird-watching, and backcountry camping
Services:	Visitor center, two information stations, and two boat-in campgrounds
Information:	P.O. Box 1369, Homestead, Florida 33090; 305-247-7275

Red mangrove forests have made the islands of Biscayne National Park natural bird sanctuaries. The dense and tangled root systems of the mangroves keep out predators that cannot fly.

Great Smoky Mountains
Heart of Appalachia

The cool moist climate of the Smokies is so pervasive that you can almost always see a soft blue haze enveloping the mountains.

Opposite: *In early October the first snowfall dusts the summit of Mount Le Conte. With an elevation of 6,593 feet, it is one of the highest mountains in the park.*

Right: *Great Fork is one of many sparkling streams that plunges down through the Smokies, creating glistening cascades and foaming rapids.*

The great forest looks like a remnant of an ancient time when the world was covered with trees, a time of constant showers, fog, and endless mist. The forest floor is thick with spongy green moss and colorful wood sorrel, and everywhere there are waterfalls cascading into nooks of rivers and streams. During the summer a riot of sound seeks your ears: the chatter of red squirrels and the calls of wrens and other birds. Great mountains rise in ridge upon rounded ridge that seem to go on and on beyond the horizon. These mountains are made of ancient rock uplifted from deep below the earth's surface and speak of much greater antiquity than the rough, craggy mountains of the western states.

The Great Smoky Mountains are the quintessential mountains of the eastern United States. Straddling the North Carolina-Tennessee border, they preserve one of the finest deciduous forests left on earth. These ancient mountains are among the oldest on the planet. The Smokies are also the highest range east of the Black Hills, and they seem strangely out of the place so far south. About 10,000 years ago, during the last Pleistocene ice age, when glaciers advanced from the north, the mountains were already millions of years old. The glaciers cooled the climate of the Great Smokies. Lured by the cold, northern evergreens and other plants extended their range south. Later, as the glaciers receded, these forests also withdrew, remaining only on the heights of the Smokies where conditions remained cool and moist. Throughout the park signs advise visitors to see "the world as it once was." Because the great glaciers were stopped in their southward journey by these mountains, which include 25 peaks above 6,000 feet, the Great Smokies today harbor a unique blend of northern and southern

animals and plants. The park is truly a vestige of an age lost in the mists of time. Northern black bears roam among a profusion of southern birds, possums, and raccoons. In the great forests, rhododendron and mountain laurel grow through narrow openings in the ancient rocks. Many of the park's nearly unbelievable variety of flowers are found only here. The vegetation is so dank and dense in some places that shrubs have taken over altogether, creating jumbled areas, called "heath balds," that are too overgrown for trees to manage to survive.

Named for the smokelike haze that constantly envelops these mountains, the Great Smokies are part of the Appalachian system. They are remarkable within the great eastern mountain chain for their wild and luxuriant vegetation. More than 100 species of trees and more than 1,300 kinds of flowering plants grow here. The incredible tangle of trees and brush throughout the park is responsible for the "smoke" that gives the mountains their name. Water and hydrocarbons are exuded in great profusion by the close-packed array of air-breathing leaves, producing the filmy haze that never leaves this place during warm weather. The park, which covers 800 square miles in the heart of these mountains, has so many types of eastern forest vegetation that it has been designated an International Biosphere Reserve. About half of this large lush forest is virgin growth that dates back to well before colonial times.

• • • • • • • • • • • • • • • • • • •

Opposite: *Sunrise barely penetrates the blanket of haze that shrouds the Smokies. Viewed from the height of Newfound Gap, the mountains reach out toward the horizon without a break.*

Summer shines through the moist chill that usually engulfs Clingmans Dome, bringing forth a short-lived but vibrant bouquet of bright wildflowers.

During May warm days dress the forest in shades of green, and flowering dogwood sparkles with its own special iridescence whenever it catches a glimmer of sunlight.

Although this is our most popular national park, it is not necessarily the most crowded. Because the park's forests and mountains are so vast and there are more than 900 miles of trails, including a 70-mile stretch of the Appalachian Trail, entire sections of the park often seem deserted. Great Smoky Mountains is almost wholly undeveloped; much of it is barely laced by paved highways or dirt roads.

Many of the coves and valleys of the Great Smoky Mountains have been settled since the late-eighteenth century, but they remained isolated and inaccessible until the twentieth century when loggers first began harvesting the virgin timber. Still preserved within the park's boundaries are many of the cabins, farmhouses, churches, and barns of the mountain people. One of the most charming of these structures is an early nineteenth-century chapel with a small graveyard.

People have not lived in Cades Cove since the first half of the century, but a white clapboard church and its silent churchyard attest to the many generations who have lived in these mountains.

Opposite: The forests of Great Smoky are a crazy quilt of hardwood and pine trees, which bespeak their individuality in autumn when their leaves glow with the entire spectrum of fall colors.

Hiking the Appalachian Trail

The Appalachian Trail, the world's longest continuous walking route, passes through 14 states, from Springer Mountain in Georgia to Mount Katahdin in Maine, along its 2,050-mile route. Hiking and trail clubs maintain shelters and campsites along the path, which was designated a national scenic trail in 1968. The trail enters Great Smoky Mountains National Park from the south through the Cheoah Mountains and the Nantahala National Forest. Most of the 70 miles of the trail, which almost perfectly bisects the park from southwest to northeast, passes through virgin wilderness well away from highways or other trails.

From the southwest the trail crosses near the 5,530-foot summit of Thunderhead Mountain and then follows the Tennessee-North Carolina border through a thick spruce and fir forest to the fire lookout tower on top of 6,643-foot Clingmans Dome, the park's highest point. From the tower and depending on the weather, hikers get either a stupendous panoramic view of range upon range of mountains or a swirl of churning clouds. After the trail crosses a park highway at Newfound Gap, hikers can take a side trip through towering 200-year-old eastern hemlocks to Alum Cave Bluffs, the site of a nineteenth-century commercial alum mine and a source of saltpeter for civil war gunpowder. After passing near the summit of 6,621-foot Mount Guyot, the trail leaves the park near Big Creek Campground and enters Cherokee National Forest.

Rising 6,643 feet, Clingmans Dome is the highest point in Tennessee. In any direction you look from the summit, you will see ridge after ridge of weather-softened, ancient mountains.

Great Smoky Mountains National Park

Established:	1934
Location:	North Carolina and Tennessee
When to go:	Open all year
Size:	520,269 acres
Terrain:	Mountains, valleys, waterfalls, and thick deciduous forests
Interesting sights:	Clingmans Dome and Thunderhead Mountain
Wildlife:	Bear, deer, raccoon, possum, fox, and salamander
Activities:	Ranger-led nature walks and children's campfire programs; auto tape tours, hiking, bicycling, fishing, horseback riding, cross-country skiing, and backpacking
Services:	Two visitor centers, park lodge, and 10 campgrounds
Information:	Gatlinburg, Tennessee 37738; 615-436-1200

Shade-loving ferns line this trail as it winds through a dense growth of tall pines on its way to a scenic overlook high on a mountaintop.

Shenandoah
The Mighty Blue Ridge

. . . .

In western Virginia, where the gentle hills and valleys of the Piedmont begin to give way to green mountain heights, there rises a great ridge. Even from a distance of many miles, it looks like an impenetrable barrier to the land that lies behind it. For many years the Blue Ridge was indeed an insurmountable obstacle to our nation's westward expansion. Its mild eastern flank sloped down to the agricultural heartland of Virginia and farther east to the burgeoning towns and cities along the Atlantic coast. Pioneers who wanted to go west from here thought twice about the ruggedness of the ridge, its height, and the fact that there were no low-lying passes through it. But the pioneers and adventurers who made it to the top of the ridge were greeted by a spectacular sight: the lovely Shenandoah Valley. This green paradise of endless forests and meadows cut by winding rivers and streams was so inviting that the valley itself seemed to hold all the promise of the West.

Shenandoah contains more artifacts of human history than most of the other national parks. It lies along a spectacular but populated section of the Blue Ridge that nearly cuts Virginia in two. Unlike most national parks, it is a place where people lived for many generations. The section of the great ridge encompassed by the park is crossed by few passes, and the imposing mountain range forced early pioneers through the Cumberland Gap and into broad Shenandoah Valley. To make this area suitable for a national park, which was mandated by Congress in 1926, the Commonwealth of Virginia acquired nearly 4,000 privately owned tracts of land in the Blue Ridge Mountains and Shenandoah Valley. The state then donated the land to the nation. No other park required the acquisition of so much private land, or required the National Park Service to

Craggy rock outcroppings on the top of Old Rag and other mountains in the Blue Ridge are composed of granite that is more than a billion years old.

Opposite: *During the green season of summer, the soft contours of the Blue Ridge are clothed in a velvety mantle of new-growth timber.*

Right: *Winter's chill clears the view from Pinnacles Overview, as lower temperatures condense the moisture in the air and the leafless trees no longer exhale the vapors that create the characteristic haze on the Blue Ridge.*

. . . .

create a park out of land that had been so widely inhabited by people. At the time it was established, much of the future parkland consisted of eroded hillsides, worn farmland, and thin second- or third-growth forests. Timber had been harvested from these woods since the early-eighteenth century. By 1935, when the park was opened to the public, nearly 2,500 mountain people had moved from their cabins and farmhouses and resettled outside the park's borders at government expense. A few mountain people continued to live in the park even after it opened, but they are all gone now.

This long, narrow park follows the Blue Ridge from the southwest to the northeast. Today the park's forests are returning; they are covering over the scars of cattle grazing, farming, and logging. The park is bisected by the Skyline Drive, which runs along the crest of the mountains for about 105 miles, with 75 overlooks and magnificent vistas of forests, mountains, and the historic Shenandoah Valley. Just off the spectacular drive are valleys filled in spring with multitudes of wildflowers. Elsewhere former pasturelands are evolving back into forests. Native animals are returning; black bears, raccoons, and opossums, America's only marsupials, now roam again as they did in pioneer days.

During the fall, when you travel the 105-mile length of the park along Skyline Drive, color dazzles your eyes at every turn in the road, as trees blaze with intense autumnal hues.

Exploring the Historic Shenandoah

Visitors to Shenandoah National Park can walk into the past by visiting the Corbin Cabin, a typical mountaineer's home. The cabin was built in 1910 by George Corbin who cut and hewed its logs. With the help of his friends, he erected the small structure. The Corbin family lived here for many years, subsisting on what they could grow or make. Today the cabin is maintained by the Potomac Appalachian Trail Club for rent to members and the public. The club also operates other rustic cabins along the Appalachian Trail.

At the Byrd Visitor Center, exhibits tell more of the story of the people who lived in these mountains from prehistoric times to the opening of the park. The park is also the home of Camp Hoover, which was President Hoover's getaway from Washington, D.C. Hoover's mandate for his retreat was fairly simple; he required his camp to be within 100 miles of the capitol, too high for mosquitos, and very close to a trout stream. Today government officials sometimes use the cabins at Camp Hoover on weekends.

Shenandoah National Park

Established:	1935
Location:	Virginia
When to go:	Open all year
Size:	195,382 acres
Terrain:	Forested mountain ridge and valleys
Interesting sight:	Corbin Cabin
Wildlife:	Bear, racoon, deer, opossum, falcon, fish, and birds
Activities:	Ranger-led nature walks; auto tours, fishing, horseback riding, bicycling, hiking, cross-country skiing, and backpacking
Services:	Two visitor centers, three park lodges, and five campgrounds
Information:	Box 348, Luray, Virginia 22835; 703-999-2243

Thomas Jefferson, whose home in Charlottesville looks out toward the Blue Ridge, much admired Dark Hollow Falls, a 70-foot cascade that flows through a rocky hollow near Big Meadows.

Mammoth Cave
Passages Beneath the Earth

Beneath the forest-covered hills of southern Kentucky, you will discover the world's largest system of caves. There are about 330 miles of underground passages on five different levels that have been explored or mapped so far. This cave is so vast and startling and its scores of passageways, rooms, and pits are so rich in history that it has been designated a United Nations World Heritage Site. The full extent of Mammoth Cave is still unknown. New caves and passageways are almost constantly being discovered, as the underground frontiers of this spectacular labyrinth extend deeper and deeper into a netherworld that almost defies belief.

People have been crawling through and living in the cave since prehistoric times. Anthropologists believe that Native Americans first discovered the great cave about 4,000 years ago. To light their way in the intense underground darkness, they fashioned torches from bundles of cane like that which still grows nearby. Charred remnants of these ancient torches have been found miles inside the cave in chambers lined with thousands upon thousands of gypsum crystals in myriad shapes. Apparently these crystals were highly valued by the early spelunkers. The cave also holds ancient footprints, undisturbed for centuries, as well as bits of clothing and abandoned sandals. Two miles from the cave entrance, the mummified body of a gypsum miner who died some 2,400 years ago has been discovered. He was crushed to death by a five-ton boulder. The man's body and his clothing are perfectly preserved and still remain in the cave.

Mammoth Cave was first discovered by white pioneers in the 1790s, and guides have been leading astonished tourists through it ever since. During the War of 1812, the cave was

The parkland is perforated with craggy sinkholes that mark places where the cave ceiling has collapsed. Water collects in the sinks where it nourishes the rapid growth of a luxuriant variety of plants and trees.

Opposite: *The steady dripping of acidic water creates stalactites that hang down from the cave's ceiling, looking like massive stone icicles.*

Right: *In the driest passages in the cave, delicate gypsum flowers blossom from the walls where water bearing gypsum evaporates quickly, leaving the crystals behind.*

mined near its entrance. Slaves did most of the work, filling large leaching vats with dirt and rock from the cave. The nitrate crystals, produced by this operation, were used to make gunpowder. Nearby in another section of the cave, off a spectacular underground passage called Broadway, there is a spot called Methodist Church where religious services are believed to have been conducted in the early 1800s. Visitors to this area today are treated to an experience much like that of earlier tourists. Cave guides turn off the lights and throw torches through the immense underground chamber, and visitors get to see with their own eyes the way the cave looked before electric lights were installed.

Booth's Amphitheater is an underground room once visited by Shakespearean actor Edwin Booth, the brother of Lincoln's assassin, John Wilkes Booth. Edwin Booth is said to have recited Hamlet's "To be or not to be" soliloquy here. Today a tape recorder eerily resonates these famous words through the cavern. Nearby is the Bottomless Pit. It was named by early guides who apparently were not able to see all the way down to the pit's bottom with the weak light of their flickering lard-oil lamps. The "bottomless hole" is actually 150 feet deep.

One of the earliest guides, Stephen Bishop, aptly described the cave as "grand, gloomy, and peculiar." He was a slave of the man who bought the cave in the 1830s, hoping to develop it as a tourist attraction. Bishop explored and mapped many of the cave's rooms and passages. His assessment of the cave is almost as accurate today as it was 150 years ago. Park officials still do not overlight the cave's interior, and visitors never lose the feeling that they are deep within the earth.

Visitors to the national park rarely see more than the 12 miles of passages that have been opened for tours. But professional spelunkers are still exploring the cave system, opening up additional passageways, many of them barely crawl spaces, and drawing new maps and charts. In 1972 a long-sought passageway was found that linked Mammoth Cave with the Flint Ridge cave system through Hanson's Lost River, an underground stream. Mammoth Cave has other subterranean waterways: Lake Lethe, the River Styx, and Echo River.

Mammoth Geology

The underground wonderland of spectacular Mammoth Cave was formed, and is still being formed, as limestone, also called calcium carbonate, dissolves in water seeping through the ground. This phenomenon is usually found where caves occur. Underneath the topsoil on the hills of southern Kentucky, there are two layers of stone. The upper is a sandstone cap that is 50 feet thick in some places. Like an umbrella, it covers the lower layer, which is a series of limestone ridges.

At places called sinkholes surface, water is able to penetrate the upper sandstone umbrella. As the water makes its way through the sandstone into the limestone, the limestone is eroded into the honeycomb of underground passageways, amphitheaters, and rooms that make up Mammoth Cave. Many of the cave's internal features such as stalagmites, stalactites, and columns are formed as the weeping water continues its work. These formations build at the rate of about one cubic inch every two centuries.

OHIO • Louisville KENTUCKY

Bowling Green ▲ Mammoth Cave

TENNESSEE

Mammoth Cave National Park

Established:	1941
Location:	Kentucky
When to go:	Open all year
Size:	52,428 acres
Terrain:	Extensive underground cave system and rolling countryside
Interesting sights:	Echo River and Bottomless Pit
Wildlife:	Cave-dwelling fish, reptiles, and insects
Activities:	Ranger-led cave tours, nature walks, and children's exploration program; fishing, horseback riding, Green River boat trips, bicycling, and backpacking
Services:	Visitor center, three campgrounds, and a park hotel
Information:	Mammoth Cave, Kentucky 42259; 502-758-2328

The sparkling travertine cascades of 75-foot-tall Frozen Niagara are flowstone, which is formed where mineral-laden water flows over a jagged heap of broken rock.

Hot Springs
An Unusual City Park

Fashioned after the palatial spas built in Europe in the nineteenth century, Bathhouse Row is now the centerpiece of Hot Springs National Park.

Opposite: *When Hernando de Soto visited the Hot Springs area in 1541, the springs in which he and his men bathed would have looked something like the Cascade, which has been restored to its natural state.*

Right: *Looking west from the observation tower, the view takes in the bustling, modern resort city of Hot Springs, which lies in a gentle valley nestled among the Zig Zag Mountains.*

Hot Springs is the smallest of all our national parks, and in many ways, it is the most unusual. Instead of covering hundreds of thousands of acres of spectacular scenery and wildlife habitat, Hot Springs is nearly surrounded by a city. And instead of protecting natural resources from commercial interests, Hot Springs National Park continues the commercial use of its major natural resource that began in the 1800s. Mineral-rich water comes bubbling forth from the park's 47 natural hot springs at the rate of nearly a million gallons a day, and the National Park Service collects, cools, and supplies hot water to commercial bathhouses both in and out of the park.

The waters of Hot Springs have long been used for medicinal purposes, first by Native Americans, then later by the Spanish explorer Hernando De Soto. He is said to have taken a hot bath here in 1541. The unique properties of the waters were investigated in 1804 under the authority of President Thomas Jefferson. In 1832 President Andrew Jackson set aside the springs as a special federal reservation. The long history of presidential interest and involvement allows park officials to refer to Hot Springs as the "oldest area in the National Park System." The government took control of the area 40 years before Yellowstone National Park was created. Throughout the nineteenth century, the town of Hot Springs prospered as a health spa, with people coming from around the world to take the waters. Entrepreneurs covered the springs and piped hot water into bathhouses along the city's main street, Central Avenue, which is also called Bathhouse Row. The elegant bathhouses that line the avenue were modeled after some of the finest spas in Europe.

Today Central Avenue is the heart of the national park. Hot Springs Mountain from which water flows at 143 degrees Fahrenheit, rises above the street. Its lower slopes were once covered by an unusual, white porous rock, called tufa, which was formed of minerals deposited by the hot water. But the slopes were altered more than a century ago when the rock was covered with tons of dirt, and professional landscapers planted shrubs, trees, and grass.

In recent years medical science has detracted from the mystique of taking hot mineral baths, which in the past were believed to cure or provide relief from such ailments as arthritis, paralysis, and gout. Today you can still enjoy a hot springwater bath at the Buckstaff, the only bathhouse operating on Bathhouse Row. The Fordyce Bathhouse is a restored spa in which visitors can see stained-glass windows, statuary, and gleaming pipes, as well as the luxurious tubs in which the aficionados of another age undertook a three-week therapy course of daily hot baths and massage.

All but two of the 47 hot springs in the park have been covered to protect the water from contamination, but here you can drink the slightly effervescent water at the place where it flows out of the earth.

Hot Springs National Park

Established:	1921
Location:	Arkansas
When to go:	Open all year
Size:	5,837 acres
Terrain:	Urban area and wooded hills
Interesting sight:	The Cascade
Activities:	Ranger-led walks, bathhouse tours, and campfire programs; hiking, horseback riding, hot baths, whirlpools, steam cabinets, hot packs, and massages
Services:	Visitor center, one campground, and six bathing facilities
Information:	P.O. Box 1860, Hot Springs, Arkansas 71902; 501-624-3383

Hot Water From the Ground

There is one hot spring in its natural condition in Hot Springs National Park. It is located a half mile above Central Avenue at the Cascade. The spring was created in 1982 by park officials who cleared away tons of dirt, decaying plants, and other materials that had collected over decades. The water flowing from the Cascade may have fallen as rain as long ago as 4,000 years and then seeped through fractures in the earth's surface. It was heated when it passed over hot, igneous rocks deep within the earth. Eventually the water returns to the surface through faults in the rock of the mountain.

The new tufa rock being created by the Cascade hot spring is building up at the rate of one inch every eight years. The bright blue-green color on the rock is algae, the only plant species that can survive in such hot water. Several concealed natural springs are located along the Tufa Terrace Trail, which is on the opposite side of the Grand Promenade from the Cascade.

ARKANSAS

• **Little Rock**

▲ **Hot Springs**

Native Americans called this place, which they considered sacred, the Valley of the Vapors, because even on hot days, the water, which comes out of the earth at 143 degrees Fahrenheit, condenses when it hits the air.

Voyageurs
Northern Lakes

Beavers are master architects and builders that carefully construct their dams and lodges, using their ax-sharp incisors and agile forepaws.

Opposite: *This chain of lakes creates a watery highway over which the voyageurs transported millions of tons of furs and trade goods in birch-bark canoes during the late-eighteenth and early-nineteenth centuries.*

Right: *Thousands of tiny islands float on the glassy surface of Rainy and Kabetogama lakes, offering refuge to a vast array of northern wildlife.*

Canoeing on a lake in Voyageurs National Park along the border of the United States and Canada, you are likely to hear the haunting cry of a loon echoing across the water. A bald eagle may describe circles high overhead. At night the eerie howls of wolves resound through the forest. Throughout this great wilderness, blue herons stride confidently on their long legs, and mallards swim in and out among the grasses near the lakeshore. Great ospreys soar through the sky; their sharp eyes scanning the water for fish. Voyageurs encom-passes a land of large lakes, with their shorelines cut by bays and inlets too numerous to count, as well as hundreds of small lakes, ponds, swamps, and one of the last remnants of the great wilderness forest that once blanketed this region.

Except for a brief gold rush in the area of Rainy Lake at the end of the nineteenth century, which left behind a mine shaft and tailings on Bushyhead Island, Voyageurs has always been wilderness. Most people who come here travel by canoe. First the Sioux and then the Chippewa paddled through the wetlands to fish, hunt, gather cranberries, or harvest wild rice. Later, during the eighteenth and nineteenth centuries, the French-Canadian voyageurs traveled through the region in large canoes piled high with tons of furs and trade goods. The voyageurs followed a route between northwest Canada and Montreal, often paddling their birch-bark canoes 16 or more hours a day. Portage, when the voyageurs were forced to carry their canoes and gear on their backs to get around water that was not navigable, was the most difficult part of their lives. The annual trading route of the voyageurs included 120 separate portages. The most arduous was a nine-mile haul over hills and through swamps; appropriately it was called Grand Portage.

A canoe in Voyageurs National Park is an open invitation to explore a myriad of bays and backwaters, islands and spits, some named and some unnamed.

• •

The route of the voyageurs, celebrated by the park's miles of waterways and portages, was so important that it was used to define the border between the United States and British-held territories in the treaty that ended the American Revolutionary War.

More than 35 percent of Voyageurs National Park is water, most of which is encompassed by four large lakes that are linked by narrow channels and small streams. There are many smaller lakes as well as marshy areas and bogs. Visitors traveling through the park today by canoe, motorboat, or houseboat often slip easily back and forth between the United States and Canada without knowing it.

Voyageurs National Park

Established:	1975
Location:	Minnesota
When to go:	Open all year. (Winter access is limited.)
Size:	218,036 acres
Terrain:	Lakes, swamps, and forest
Interesting sight:	Locator Lake
Wildlife:	Bald eagle, osprey, loon, beaver, heron, and wolf
Activities:	Ranger-led walks and canoe trips; canoeing, boating, camping, hiking, fishing, swimming, water-skiing, snowmobiling, cross-country skiing, snowshoeing, and ice fishing
Services:	Three visitor centers, park lodge, two hotels, and backcountry boat-in campsites
Information:	P.O. Box 50, International Falls, Minnesota 56649; 218-283-9821

A Trip to Locator Lake

A ranger-led trip from the Kabetogama Lake Visitor Center to Locator Lake is good way for visitors to get to know some of the natural delights of Voyageurs National Park. No other national park offers this kind of tour. The weekly trip includes travel by boat, canoe, and on foot. A boat takes visitors across Kabetogama Lake to a dock near La Bontys Point. From there you walk on a two-mile trail through a spruce bog and past a fascinating beaver dam and lodge. After you climb the ridge, the trail drops down through pine trees to the shore of Locator Lake. The park service keeps several canoes cached at the lake. With a ranger in the lead, visitors board canoes and paddle around the lovely woodland lake. The reward for this effort is the chance to see bald eagles, loons, ospreys, blue-winged teal, and occasionally, herons.

ONTARIO

Voyageurs

International Falls

Duluth •

MINNESOTA

Minneapolis •

WISCONSIN

These rich wetlands provided first the Sioux and later the Chippewa with an abundance of fish and game, as well as a rich harvest of crimson cranberries and sumptuous wild rice.

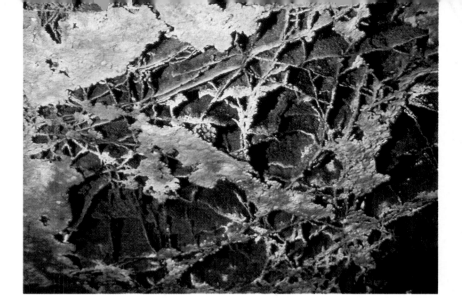

Wind Cave
Caverns of Limestone

· ·

The artistry of trickling water is almost complete in Wind Cave because the water table has now fallen below the level of the cave-forming limestone, bringing to a close aeons of natural sculpting.

Opposite: *This rolling landscape of prairie and woodland gives no clues to the complex labyrinth of highly decorated caverns that lies below its surface.*

Right: *The lacy boxwork in Wind Cave was created when water carrying dissolved crystals of calcium carbonate seeped through a network of cracks.*

Buffalo, pronghorn antelope, and mule deer still roam the grassy hills of the Great Plains in South Dakota. Overhead prairie falcons circle, looking for prey. To the northwest, the eastern flank of the pine-covered Black Hills looms in the distance. But this tranquil world of prairie grass and sunshine is somewhat deceptive. Below the vast prairie, there is a great underground wonderland, where nature is putting on a spectacular display of geological artisanship.

Wind Cave is one of the largest caverns in the world, a labyrinth of passages carved out of limestone beds that have existed for 60 million years. Unlike many limestone caverns, including Mammoth Cave, that formed at relatively shallow depths sometimes less than 100 feet, Wind Cave twists and turns its way through rock hundreds of feet below the surface; in one place the cavern is more than 600 feet below the surface. The cave gets its name from the strong air currents that blow alternately in and out of the caverns. The direction of the wind depends on whether the air pressure in the cave is higher or lower than the atmospheric pressure outside the cave. In a very real sense, the cave is breathing, and this constant rush of air, first in and then out, keeps the interior of the great cavern drier than most other caves. In Wind Cave you won't hear the eerie sound of endlessly dripping and seeping water.

Because Wind Cave is not as wet as many caves, there are almost no stalactites and stalagmites. Nature has worked a different kind of underground magic here. Instead of flowing through wide openings and depositing minerals in thick columns, water from the surface seeped through tiny cracks and

· ·

pores in the limestone. This seepage deposited a thin film, along with tiny droplets, on the walls and ceilings, creating a unique geological spectacle. Stunning multicolored encrustations decorate the walls and ceilings throughout the cavern. Descriptive names explain the character of these startling works of nature. One kind of formation is called popcorn, a knobby growth that looks like splotches of coral of every size and shape. Another is called frostwork; it varies in size from small strands to large round formations that resemble snowballs. Wind Cave is probably most famous for what is undoubtedly the world's finest display of boxwork, a calcite formation resembling honeycomb. Boxwork is found everywhere in the cave, but the best examples are in the subterranean chambers called the Post Office, the Temple, and the Pearly Gates.

In 1881 two brothers, Jesse and Tom Bingham, discovered this unique underground realm of wonders. Tom was chasing a wounded antelope in a ravine when he heard a loud whistling noise. As he looked down, his hat was blown off his head by a powerful wind blowing directly out of a crack in the rocks. The brothers brought people to see the cave's wonders, and everyone who saw it seemed to want to develop it for a profit. Several groups, one of them calling itself the Wonderful Wind Cave Improvement Company, competed for the right to mine the cave and lead tourists through it. In 1903 the federal government ended years of fierce bickering by establishing Wind Cave as a national park. It was the first cavern to be brought into the park system.

Formation of Wind Cave

Roughly 335 million years ago, a shallow sea covered South Dakota. At that time North America was located on the earth's equator, and its climate was tropical. Gradually the sea's water level dropped as the land rose and moved north. A layer of sediment grew to a thickness of between 300 and 600 feet. About 320 million years ago, another sea inundated this area, depositing another layer of sediment several hundred feet thick on top of the first one. The forces that lifted the Black Hills created cracks in these limestone layers. Over a time span of millions of years, water seeped into these cracks, gradually dissolving the rock and creating the labyrinth of passages and chambers that we see now.

An unusual ecosystem also extends across the land above the cave. This area marks the boundary between the prairie and the ponderosa pine forests of the Black Hills. The grassland here is inhabited by prairie birds, such as falcons and meadowlarks, as well as nuthatches and wild turkeys that come from the forests.

SOUTH DAKOTA

• Pierre

Rapid City
•

▲ Wind
Cave

Sioux Falls •

Clusters of white aragonite and calcite crystals bejewel the walls and ceilings of Wind Cave where they were formed by the unique geology of the region.

Opposite: At one time 60 million buffalo spread out across the vast open land of the American West; now small protected herds, like this one, bespeak the magnificence of those lost multitudes.

Wind Cave National Park

Established:	1903
Location:	South Dakota
When to go:	Open all year
Size:	28,292 acres
Terrain:	Grassland prairie and underground caverns
Interesting sights:	The Post Office and boxwork throughout the cave
Wildlife:	Buffalo, pronghorn antelope, elk, deer, prairie dog, falcon, meadowlark, wild turkey, and nuthatch
Activities:	Ranger-led cave tours and campfire talks; scenic drives, nature trails, hiking, bicycling, and backpacking
Services:	Visitor center, exhibits, and one campground
Information:	Rt. 1 Box 190-WCNP, Hot Springs, South Dakota 57747; 605-745-4600

Badlands
Fantasyland

· · · · · · · · · · · · · · · · · · · ·

This rock was carefully balanced on a spire as erosion gradually removed the softer layers of sandstone from beneath the hard caprock.

Opposite: *Bands of soft colors recall the long history of a plain that was relatively quickly eroded by the powerful forces of wind and water into the tortured sculpture of the Badlands.*

Right: *Dawn slips slowly into the Badlands, highlighting the towering heights of castles, buttresses, and pinnacles with morning's pale light.*

Astunning amalgamation of rock spires, castles, cathedrals, and battlements, almost a hundred miles long and fifty miles wide, cuts across the Great Plains of southwestern South Dakota. But you can walk or drive across the rolling grasslands almost to its borders without being aware that this vast expanse of otherworldly terrain is nearby. Then suddenly, in a matter of a few yards, you are amid a theatrical and bewildering jumble of towers and imposing buttresses. Rock palaces, hundreds of feet high, loom large against big prairie sky. The terrain of the area is so arid and the land formations so eerie that the Sioux called this place *mako sica,* or "bad land." French-Canadian trappers called the area *les mauvaises terres à traverser,* or "bad lands to cross."

Early pioneers avoided the Badlands, but people have lived among these otherworldly formations for millennia. Within Badlands National Park more than 80 archaeological sites have been discovered. They indicate that the first humans arrived in the area as long as 7,000 years ago. These people were probably nomadic hunters and gatherers and may have been among the early arrivals from Asia across the Bering land bridge.

In more recent times, the Dakotas, more commonly called the Sioux, were masters of the northern plains. During the last years of their wars with the United States, they used the remote Badlands as their stronghold against the U.S. Army. In the late 1880s, the Sioux adopted a mystical religious movement called the Ghost Dance. Other tribes, such as the Comanche who were making a last stand against encroaching white settlers on the southern plains, also embraced these beliefs. The Ghost Dance ceremony, which could take days to perform, promised

· ·

that the white farmers and ranchers would disappear and that the buffalo would return. The ritual was outlawed by the U.S. government, but for many years the Sioux danced without interference in the Badlands. The last Ghost Dance took place in 1890 on Stronghold Table just a few days before more than 150 followers of Big Foot, chief of the Miniconjou Sioux, were massacred by U.S. troops at Wounded Knee, 25 miles to the south. Today Stronghold Table is at the end of a long rutted road that winds through lonely grassland. It is a haunting place that seems to be alive with the memories of this last dance before the final defeat and capitulation.

Despite the unfavorable reputation of the Badlands in the nineteenth century, at least one early visitor was fascinated by this stark and angry landscape eroded out of the surface of the prairie. In 1848 Fray Pierre-Jean DeSmet wrote: "Viewed at a distance, these lands exhibit the appearance of extensive villages and ancient castles." People visiting the park today are likely to get the same impression, especially when they look at the park's most monumental geological formation, the Wall. Dividing the northern grasslands from those in the south that are about 200 feet lower in elevation, the great Badlands Wall extends for 100 miles. This multitude of fantastic pinnacles, spires, pillars, shelves, and chimneys is an immense natural barrier cutting through the landscape. The Wall is almost impossible to see from the northern plains, but it rises above the southern plains like an ancient and abandoned city skyline.

In the Badlands water is the force that sculpts the land, but this powerful element is assisted by wind that "sandblasts" the stone with airborne grit and dust. An annual cycle of freeze and thaw also contributes to the ongoing creation of the Wall, which is occurring at a phenomenal rate, geologically speaking. Photographs taken just 50 years ago show different formations than those seen today; this is the result of unusually rapid erosion. Measurements by geologists confirm that the Wall's surface is wearing away at an almost unbelievably fast pace; in some places an inch or more is removed from the surface each year.

Badlands Geology

Badlands are found in many parts of the world. This kind of geological formation usually occurs in semiarid climates and is characterized by countless gullies and ridges, and sparse vegetation. The term "badlands" was first used to describe the area of South Dakota that is the world's most extensive and best example of this kind of topography. The Badlands are cut from deep alluvial and volcanic ash deposits that have been sculptured and carved into fantastic forms of every shape and size by the continuous action of wind and water falling in infrequent but torrential downpours.

It all began about 80 million years ago when the Pierre shale, the bottom layer of the Badlands geology, was laid down by a great inland sea. About 35 million years ago, rivers and streams running downhill from the Black Hills spread sand, mud, and gravel on the area. Volcanic activity, probably in the Rocky Mountains to the west, poured vast quantities of wind-borne ash on the plains of South Dakota. For a few more million years, the land built up faster than it was eroded away. Then the balance changed, and wind and water went to work to create the geological wonderland we see today.

Only native grasses can survive in the Badlands' extreme temperatures, which range from 110 degrees Fahrenheit in summer to 30 below zero in winter.

A winter sunset washes this otherworldly landscape with a warm pink glow that contours the harsh terrain, creating an impression of the Badlands as a natural sculpture garden.

Today, with the Sioux defeated and the pioneers long gone, the Wall is the picturesque backdrop for a herd of buffalo. The animals were reintroduced into the area in 1963 after having been nearly exterminated by white hunters in the nineteenth century. Also wandering on the endless grasslands are lovely and graceful pronghorn antelope. Rocky Mountain bighorn sheep were brought to Badlands in 1964, and coyotes roam throughout the park. Other animals that once lived here—the grizzly bear, gray wolf, and American elk—are all gone today.

Gone for an even longer time are such creatures as the titanothere, an early ancestor of the horse that was about 12 feet tall and fed on prairie grasses millions of years ago. Some of the world's richest fossil beds are located in the Badlands. The remains of hundreds of prehistoric animals have been found, including an ancestor of the camel; a sheeplike creature with three horns, called the protoceras; and the fierce saber-toothed tiger.

The Badlands is a unique region, rich in history and geology. Someone once said: "It's a good place that's gotten a bad name." Anyone who appreciates a surprising and unusual land of rare natural beauty will agree.

Badlands National Park

Established:	1978
Location:	South Dakota
When to go:	Open all year
Size:	243,244 acres
Terrain:	Badlands and prairie
Interesting sight:	The Wall
Wildlife:	Buffalo, pronghorn antelope, mule deer, coyote, prairie dog, Rocky Mountain bighorn sheep, and prairie rattlesnake
Activities:	Ranger-led nature walks and fossil demonstrations; hiking and backpacking
Services:	Two visitor centers, two campgrounds, and a park lodge
Information:	P.O. Box 6, Interior, South Dakota 57750; 605-433-5361

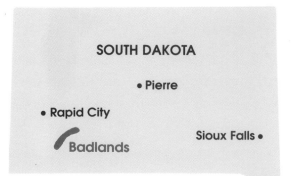

Hiking the Wall

The Windows Overlook is the trailhead for three nature walks, each of which gives visitors an excellent look at a unique piece of Badlands' geology by leading them into different sections of the Wall. The Door Trail takes you just a few steps through a notch in the wall and onto what seems like the surface of the moon: a tangle of wildly eroded and barren hills that is the heart of Badlands.

Even more spectacular, the Notch Trail winds up the Wall to a window, or notch, eroded out of the top of a cliff. It faces southwest toward Cliff Shelf and Cedar Pass. At one point on the trail, you must climb straight up a wooden ladder on the face of a claystone cliff. The view is wonderful: prairie and badlands, the White River, and in the distance, the Pine Ridge Indian Reservation. Almost equally beautiful, the Windows Trail leads to a spectacular natural window in the Wall that overlooks an unexpectedly deep canyon cut into the tableland.

Rain turns the Wall into a gooey mess of gray clay so slippery that it often cannot support its own weight, causing pieces of the cliffs to slide off.

Gradually all evidence of ranching and farming is being erased from Badlands National Park, and a thick carpet of grasses and wildflowers is spreading out across the landscape, slowing the rush of erosion.

Theodore Roosevelt
Where the West Begins

Erosion of the tumbled rocky badlands in Wind Canyon in the South Unit was accelerated by wind working in tandem with the dynamic force of water.

Opposite: *The parkland today looks much as it did when Teddy Roosevelt lived here in the 1880s. Now as then, the landscape has the "curious, fantastic beauty" that T.R. so much enjoyed.*

Right: *Flowing northward toward the Missouri River, the Little Missouri winds through the rugged badlands and green valley it has cut through the prairie.*

Theodore Roosevelt first arrived in Dakota Territory in 1883, just a few years after the end of the war between the Dakota tribes, or the Sioux as they are called more often, and the U.S. Army. Roosevelt came to bag a buffalo, but he ended up trying his hand at running cattle in the last years of open-range ranching. Soon after his arrival, the buffalo became almost extinct, and unusually severe winters in 1886 and 1887 brought the cattle boom to a close. Roosevelt emerged from his experiences in the West a changed man; he had become a dedicated conservationist and went on to become the political leader who did more for our national park system than anyone else before or since.

Theodore Roosevelt National Park is a surprisingly rugged landscape that stretches along the Little Missouri River. Here you can't help but feel a haunting sense of the Old West. This austere landscape of rolling prairie cut by rivers and streams provides a habitat for an astonishing array of wildlife. Along with buffalo, elk, white-tailed and mule deer, and pronghorn antelope, there are wild horses and mountain lions, as well as millions of prairie dogs and other small mammals, reptiles, and amphibians. The theme song of the park is the call of the western meadowlark; it is a bright flutelike sound that is unmistakable.

Today the park includes significant portions of the Little Missouri badlands, along with an important grassland area, which has such abundant animal life that it looks like an African veldt; and sections of the ranch property that once belonged to T.R. In the spring, when it is rainy, a spectacular bouquet made up of multitudes of wildflowers colors the river's bottomland and the grassy flats. This is an uncrowded land, far removed from large urban centers. It is a place where visitors can experience the West and get used to lovely solitude in much the same way that young Teddy Roosevelt must have more than a century ago. The prairie dog towns still bustle, eagles soar proudly through the sky, and stunning, seemingly endless sunsets brighten the evening sky. Little has changed.

The park is divided into two units about 60 miles apart. The park headquarters is in the town of Medora in the South Unit. Rich in the history and lore of the frontier, Medora was founded by a French nobleman, the marquis de Mores, who named the town after his wife. His 27-room prairie chateau broods over Medora from a bluff across the river— silent testimony to a place and age rapidly receding into the depths of time. In sharp contrast to this grand house, the visitor center is located in the rustic cabin that was once the headquarters for T.R.'s cattle operation, the Maltese Cross Ranch. The cabin has been moved from its original site seven miles south. Roosevelt lived in the cabin in 1884 and 1885. From Medora Overlook above town, visitors view the town as it might have appeared in Roosevelt's day.

Opposite: *The red band that runs through the center of this bluff is Badlands scoria. This natural red brick resembles volcanic rock, but it was baked by heat from a burning vein of soft coal.*

In 1883 Roosevelt purchased a share in the Maltese Cross Ranch. He and his partners did not actually own the land; for their money they got this cabin, some cattle, brands, and squatter's rights.

76

If the South Unit is more historic, the North Unit may be more scenic and wild. Smaller than the South Unit and less closely associated with Roosevelt, the North Unit contains most of the park's wilderness. This part of the park gives visitors the feeling they have entered an earlier era when civilization was farther away. Here the Little Missouri winds its spectacular course through rugged badlands where the cliffs seem higher, the canyons deeper, and the colored striations on the eroded rock more pronounced than elsewhere in this vast prairie wilderness. Oxbow Overlook provides a fine view of the Little Missouri River; it is a stunning vista with the blue river cutting through extensive badlands on either side. Longhorn steers were brought to the park to commemorate the thousands and thousands of longhorns that were driven from Texas to the nearby Long-X Ranch more than a century ago. They graze on the sagebrush flats in this place where the Old West is still alive.

Geology of the Continent's Center

The history of North Dakota's badlands and prairie goes back about 65 million years. As the Rocky Mountains rose up over the Great Plains, streams began to erode the peaks, carrying their sediment eastward and spreading mountain debris over the plains. Later, between five and 10 million years ago, the entire great plains were lifted up, and the Little Missouri River began to carve its badlands. The river's many small tributaries reshaped nearby areas.

The result of this continuous process of deposition of sediment and erosion by water is spectacular. There are wildly corrugated cliffs, twisted gullies, and rugged pinnacles. Dome-shaped hills, with layers of rock and sediment forming colored horizontal striations, run for miles and miles. This wild region is the same today as when Theodore Roosevelt described the place as "a chaos of peaks, plateaus, and ridges."

Theodore Roosevelt National Park

Established:	1978
Location:	North Dakota
When to go:	Open all year. (Winter access is limited.)
Size:	70,416 acres
Terrain:	Grassland prairie and badlands
Interesting sights:	Elkhorn Ranch and Roosevelt's cabin
Wildlife:	Buffalo, deer, elk, pronghorn antelope, wild horse, mountain lion, prairie dog, meadowlark, small mammals, and snakes
Activities:	Ranger-led walks, talks, tours of T.R.'s Maltese Cross cabin, and evening campfire programs; hiking, horseback riding, auto tours, canoeing, float trips, fishing, cross-country skiing, snowmobiling, and backpacking
Services:	Three visitor centers and two campgrounds
Information:	P.O. Box 7, Medora, North Dakota 58645; 701-623-4466

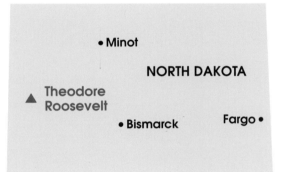

The summit of this column of pale gray clay is protected by its hard caprock, but over time, wind and water erosion will narrow the pillar until it eventually collapses.

At Oxbow Overlook in the North Unit, you look out across the canyon of the Little Missouri across a landscape tinted blue green by the ubiquitous sagebrush.

Rocky Mountain
Atop the Mighty Divide

. . . .

These bright, delicate flowers belie the incredible toughness of plants that survive in the alpine tundra, buffeted by drying winds and further challenged by rapid temperature changes.

Opposite: *More than half of the 50 highest mountain peaks in the United States are in the Colorado Rockies, and many of these giants are encompassed by Rocky Mountain National Park.*

Right: *In autumn the leaves of the aspens along the Continental Divide become golden disks that glimmer in the lengthening rays of the sun.*

This is high country, with sweeping vistas of a jagged skyline crowned by towering summits. Snow lingers here year round, and the highest cirques preserve remnants of glaciers leftover from the last ice age. In Rocky Mountain National Park, there are 78 peaks that are more than 12,000 feet high; 18 of them reach above 13,000 feet. Contrasting with this jagged terrain, meadows come alive in spring and summer as wildflowers poke their way through the tundra. This park makes accessible a vast wonderland of alpine terrain, towering peaks, high mountain tarns, and glacial moraines. "Of all the large and rugged mountain ranges in the world, these are the most friendly, the most hospitable," wrote pioneer naturalist Enos Mills, who was instrumental in the creation of Rocky Mountain National Park in 1915. In the southern Rockies, the summers are fairly long, the valleys are broad and inviting, and the mountains are crisscrossed by trails and roads left by miners a century ago, which makes these mountains more affable than other American ranges.

With the highest average elevation of any national park, including those in Alaska, Rocky Mountain sits atop the Continental Divide, the great ridge of mountains that cuts the continental United States in two. Water on the east side of the divide flows to the Atlantic Ocean, and water on the west side ultimately makes its way to the Pacific. Much of the parkland is above the timberline, which is about 11,500 feet high in this section of the Rockies. The park's centerpiece, Trail Ridge Road,

. . . .

is the nation's highest highway and leads into the heart of a spectacular alpine world. One stunning 10-mile stretch of the road follows a ridge as it rises to 12,000 feet.

In many ways the timberline, which is so evident from this dramatic drive, is a biological battle line. Just below the timberline, such hearty trees as subalpine firs, limber pines, and Engelmann spruce struggle upwards root by root to find room in which to grow and survive. Above the last trees, an even harsher world challenges the survival of the most robust plants, which cling tenuously to life during a brief growing season and in the face of constant winds. Here are lovely meadows bathed in green grasses and awash with dozens of species of wildflowers that grow low to the ground for protection in this harsh environment.

The park is not just a land of tundra, high rocky places, and ceaseless wind. Below the timberline, you will find lovely hidden spots, such as the sublimely beautiful Dream Lake, a rock-rimmed mountain pond nestled in a meadow at the foot of rugged 12,713-foot Hallet Peak. Countless numbers of wild creatures wander through the woods and meadows. Mule deer and black bears are common sights, and beavers build their dams in many of the streams that drain the lake. Higher up are elk, while higher still on seemingly impossible vertical cliffs and safe from predators are elusive Rocky Mountain bighorn sheep, appropriately the symbol of this alpine park.

• •

Like most lakes in the Rockies, Bear Lake is a brilliant blue tarn that was scooped out by glaciers during the last ice age.

Right: *It is difficult to imagine a more perfectly appropriate name for Dream Lake, which sparkles in an idyllic setting at the foot of towering Hallet Peak.*

Longs Peak is the park's tallest mountain, measuring 14,225 feet. This jagged peak was sheared off by glaciers moving down from its summit.

Climbing Longs Peak

At 14,255 feet, Longs Peak, a steep-sided mountain with a flat top, dominates the Front Range of the Colorado Rockies for almost 100 miles. Along with Pikes Peak to the south, it is one of the landmark peaks of the range and one of America's most distinctive mountains. Some of the most difficult climbing routes in North America lead up the peak's eastern face, a 90-degree cliff that is more than 2,500-feet high. There are also walking routes to the summit. The most popular of these is the East Longs Peak Trail, which begins at the Longs Peak ranger station. The eight-mile trail climbs nearly 5,000 feet, or almost a mile up. At first it passes through a forest of windblown limber pines, then across a rugged boulder field above the timberline where the real work begins. After scrambling through a notch called the Keyhole, hikers traverse a rock field then head up a steep granite slab, called the Homestretch, which leads to the summit. The top, which is five acres across, is surprisingly level. From here, on a clear day, the views of the peaks of Rocky Mountain National Park and the mountains beyond seem endless.

WYOMING
• Cheyenne

Rocky
▲ Mountains
Boulder •   • Denver

COLORADO

Rocky Mountain National Park

Established:	1915
Location:	Colorado
When to go:	Open all year. (Winter access is limited.)
Size:	265,193 acres
Terrain:	Alpine peaks and valleys
Interesting sights:	Dream Lake and Longs Peak
Wildlife:	Bear, Rocky Mountain bighorn sheep, mule deer, elk, beaver, marmot, and cougar
Activities:	Ranger-led nature and history walks, campfire talks, and snowshoe walks; hiking, horseback trail rides, bicycling, fishing, rock and mountain climbing, cross-country and downhill skiing, snowshoeing, snowmobiling, and backpacking
Services:	Three visitor centers, museum, and five campgrounds
Information:	Estes Park, Colorado 80517, 303-586-2371

Trail Ridge Road is a modern highway along an ancient trail that climbs from Estes Park to the crest of the Front Range, crosses over the Continental Divide, and then descends to Grand Lake.

Grand Teton
Awesome Mountain

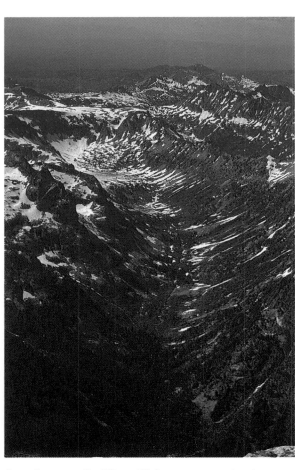

From the summit of Grand Teton, you can clearly see the U shape of the north fork of Cascade Canyon that was gouged out by glaciers during the most recent ice ages.

Opposite: *At the end of Cascade Canyon, the clear, cool water of Jenny Lake mirrors the magnificent snowy peaks of the Cathedral Group.*

Right: *Rising abruptly out of Jackson Hole, Grand Teton and its craggy attendant mountains touch the clouds that hover above them in the bright blue Wyoming sky.*

The Tetons are the mountains of dreams, a rise of granite towers so impossible and impenetrable that they appear to guard a hidden land that only can be imagined but never attained. The summit of Grand Teton is 13,770 feet above sea level, and the mountain shoots a mile and a half straight up into the Wyoming sky without intervening foothills. Flanked by stunning spires, pinnacles, and buttes, the steepness of Grand Teton is breathtaking.

An early nineteenth-century French trapper supposedly named the Tetons for female breasts, which he imagined they resembled. The name does not really fit, but for English-speaking Americans it has taken on a haunting and descriptive quality that seems to go with the mountains. Not particularly large, at 485 square miles, Grand Teton National Park encompasses the 6,300-foot-high valley called Jackson Hole, with Yellowstone on the north and the Tetons on the west. Within the park's boundaries, there is more scenery, more history, more animals, more boating and fishing, and more hiking and mountain climbing than in many areas twice its size. The Grand Teton massif, which includes five consort peaks, Middle and South Tetons, Mount Owen, Teewinot, and Nez Perce, dominates the central part of the range. To the north Mount Moran is a stark granite hulk 12,605 feet high. It rises in splendid isolation from the shore of Jackson Lake, the largest of six jewellike lakes strung along the base of the mountains.

Many people who visit the Tetons are surprised at their first sight of these rugged mountains. They are hypnotically alluring. There are no bad views of them from any place in the park. Most visitors also find that they are familiar with these mountains. They have already seen them in western movies, such as *Shane*, and in countless cigarette and jeans commercials. Grand Teton has become a recognizable symbol of the long gone American West—free, proud, and lonesome.

The Snake River flows peacefully from Jackson Lake. The 30-mile-long river is braided into several channels that run through a forested, serpentine trough cut by the river into the floor of Jackson Hole. It is an ideal stream for first-time river runners. Their ride down the Snake gives them a unique perspective on some of America's most spectacular scenery. Wildlife flourishes in the valley of the Snake. Bald eagles nest in dead trees alongside the stream, as do the ospreys that cruise above the river casting their sharp eyes for native cutthroat trout that is their favorite meal. In little side streams, moose often wade up to their knees as they placidly feed on grasses along the shore or nibble on lily pads. Along the banks otters play, while beavers go about their business of dam building in watery alcoves and nooks.

• •

Hiking to Lake Solitude

A spectacular hike up through a deep slice in the mountains, called Cascade Canyon, just north of Grand Teton, gives visitors a good feel for some of the geological wonders of the park. The hike starts on the west side of Jenny Lake. In the lower part of the canyon, rushing water, here and there in the form of cascading falls, seems to be constantly at work, eating away at the granite walls. Cascade Canyon originally was cut as a V by running water. Now it has been formed into a U shape; its nearly vertical sides sculpted by the powerful activity of glaciers in the last ice age.

As you walk through a series of switchbacks, granite walls rise 2,000 to 3,000 feet above you. Two miles into the canyon, the peaks tower a mile above. Abruptly the canyon drops away, the rocky trail begins a steeper ascent into a broad bowl, and you discover that you have walked around to the north side of Grand Teton. After a total of seven miles, you arrive at Lake Solitude. Here, in an incredibly beautiful valley, the air is intoxicatingly clear, and wildflowers, such as pink primrose and St. John's wort, abound. Grand Teton and Mount Owen are reflected in the lake, and a circular granite wall rises in the west.

The silvery Snake River catches the late-afternoon sun as it meanders along its course, flowing south out of Yellowstone on its way to join the mighty Columbia.

Teton Geology

The fierce geology of the Tetons accounts for almost everything unusual about the region: the afternoon thunderstorms that can turn suddenly nasty, the deep canyons that shelter deer and bear, the broad river basin that provides grazing for moose and a refuge for elk in winter, and the long and bitter winters. A walk into any of the canyons between the mountains reveals this geology firsthand. The Tetons are a text-book example of fault-block mountains. This means that they were pushed up as the earth split along a north-south fault line. As pressures deep within the mantle forced the blocks on each side of the crack together, the western block rose to form the mountains and the eastern block sank to the form the valley.

The granite on the summits of some of the peaks is more than three billion years old, which makes it some of the oldest rock in North America. But the mountains themselves are the youngest of the Rocky Mountains. They are mere adolescents that are only 12 million years old, compared with the rest of the 60-million-year-old range. Because of their relative youth, the Tetons are more rugged than the rest of the Rockies. Since their eastern flank was the side that shoved up, this side of the mountains is more abrupt and dramatic than the somewhat gentler western side. This accounts for the fact that you have probably heard of Jackson Hole but may not know about Driggs, the Idaho town at the western base of the Tetons in a broad valley known as Pierre's Hole.

On stormy days with dark, mean clouds swirling around their summits and mist drifting up the canyons between them, the Tetons look like they are slow dancing in the hall of the mountain king.

Right: The lakes in Grand Teton reflect images of the intensely blue sky and the grandeur of the surrounding mountains from the depths of their crystal-clear water.

The first people arrived in Jackson Hole long before white men set foot on the North American continent. A pointed obsidian blade found in the northern end of the park indicates a human presence as long ago as 8,500 years. The first humans who came here were probably hunters and gatherers. By 1600 Shoshone and Athabaskan people had discovered the valley. In 1807 a member of the Lewis and Clark expedition, John Colter, wandered alone into the Yellowstone-Jackson Hole area and brought back tales of geysers and impenetrable mountains. The region was first named "Colter's Hell" in his honor. The first permanent settlers arrived in the 1880s. One homestead has been maintained in the park, a log ranch house built by the Cunningham family on the eastern side of Jackson Hole. The view of the Grand Teton through its kitchen window is a stunning reminder of the hardships and terrible winters the family endured beneath the same spectacular scenery.

To many park visitors, the Tetons resemble an immense gothic cathedral, rising a mile and a half into the azure sky of northwest Wyoming.

Grand Teton National Park

Established:	1929
Location:	Wyoming
When to go:	Open all year. (Winter access is limited.)
Size:	310,516 acres
Terrain:	Mountains, canyons, lakes, and river valley
Interesting sights:	Cunningham Cabin and Lake Solitude
Wildlife:	Black and grizzly bear, moose, elk, deer, cutthroat trout, bald eagle, osprey, beaver, and otter
Activities:	Ranger-led nature walks, slide talks, campfire programs, tepee demonstrations, and wildlife watches; raft trips, mountain climbing, bicycling, horseback riding, fishing, ice fishing, dogsledding, cross-country skiing, and backpacking
Services:	Two visitor centers, three lodges and cabins, two guest ranches, and eight campgrounds.
Information:	Post Office Drawer 170, Moose, Wyoming 83012; 307-733-2880

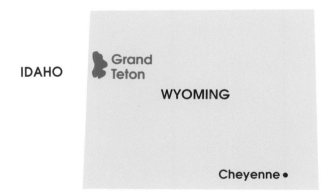

• Billings

MONTANA

IDAHO

Grand Teton

WYOMING

Cheyenne •

The moose that wades out to nibble on this luxuriant growth of water plants and the kingfisher that comes here to fish must thank the beaver for felling the aspens that grow nearby to dam this pond.

Glacier
Sculpted by Ice

. . . .

Summer melt from the park's 50 glaciers guarantees a steady supply of cascading water for Appekunny Falls, one of Glacier's extensive assortment of waterfalls.

Opposite: *The horn atop Mount Clements (8,774 feet high) was created when three or more glaciers assaulted the mountain, shearing away everything but this rocky pyramid.*

Right: *When the warming climate stopped the forward momentum of a glacier here, it dumped some of the rocky debris it has gathered, creating the terminal moraine that formed St. Mary Lake.*

Glacier National Park presents the Rocky Mountains as you have always imagined them: granite peaks with glimmering glaciers fitted into their gorges, fields run riot with wildflowers, lakes as deep and blue as the summer sky, cascading waterfalls, grizzly bears, wooded slopes, and miles and miles of wilderness trails. The park is the southern section of the Waterton-Glacier International Peace Park, which the United States shares with Canada. It is adorned with 200 lakes and drained by 936 miles of rivers and streams. The park is made even more magnificent by two especially graceful ranges of the northern Rockies and dozens of glaciers that seem to flow down every high mountain valley.

Glacier's 1,600 square miles, which make it almost as large as the state of Delaware, offer "the best care-killing scenery on the continent," in the words of pioneer naturalist John Muir. The mountains of Glacier are not especially high when compared with those in other national parks in the Rockies. But dramatic contrasts in elevation give the park a special kind of grandeur. A stunning example is the abrupt rise from the surface of Lake McDonald at 3,153 feet to the summit of Mount Cleveland at 10,466 feet. Adding to the special beauty of Glacier is the distinctive and unusually beguiling quality of the sheer faces and angular contours of the multicolored peaks with their flanks covered by heavy forests.

The area's sheltered valleys and bountiful wildlife have lured people here for more than 8,000 years. Ancient tribes tracked buffalo across the plains, fished the mountain lakes, and crossed the high passes. The Blackfeet, whose reservation adjoins the park to the east, controlled the region during the eighteenth

. . . .

and most of the nineteenth centuries. Straddling the Continental Divide in northern Montana, Glacier remains today an unspoiled yet accessible wilderness.

An east-west scenic highway that is one of the most spectacular drives in the United States crosses the park. Called the Going-to-the-Sun Road, it provides a highlight tour of the park's major attractions: lovely McDonald Lake, which is 10 miles long and the park's largest lake; McDonald Falls; Avalanche Creek, where there is a trail-head for a self-guided nature walk; the precipitous Garden Wall, a section of the Continental Divide created by glaciers on both sides of its ridge; Logan Pass, atop the divide; the lovely Hanging Garden Walk; and Jackson Glacier. For further exploration of this stunning wilderness realm, there are more than 700 miles of trails for hiking and horseback riding. On the trails you can travel alone for an hour, several days, or longer among some of the continent's most splendid scenery. If you can find the time, you might want to follow John Muir's advice "Give a month at least to this precious reserve. The time will not be taken from the sum of your life. Instead . . . it will make you truly immortal."

Glacier Geology

The remnants of dozens of glaciers still cling to the walls of great rock amphitheaters, which are called cirques, in the mountains of Glacier National Park. At lower elevations glaciers have carved out the landscape of the park from layers of sedimentary rock, consisting of mudstone, sandstone, and limestone. The park's two chief mountain ranges, the Livingston and the Lewis, form the backbone of Glacier. They began to be thrust up about 60 million years ago. Still active today, erosion in the form of wind, rain, snow, and flash floods started working on these ranges about 50 million years ago. But the major carving of the mountains started about three million years ago with the Pleistocene epoch, during which four distinct glacial periods occurred. The last of these ice ages took place only 10,000 years ago. The area of the park once contained 90 glacial remnants of this last ice age, but today only about 50 remain. Two of the glaciers, Grinnell and Sperry, are easily accessible to hikers. Each is about 300 acres in size, and both are tucked into high shady hanging valleys where they continue their work of sculpturing mountains, valleys, and lakes.

Water from this glacier-fed stream near Sperry Glacier, the park's biggest, will gradually wear away the sharpness of these rocks, continuing the contouring begun by ice.

Glacier lilies and other summer wildflowers paint the alpine tundra with bright colors near a part of the Lewis Range of the Rocky Mountains known as the Garden Wall.

Plants and Animals

Glacier's climate is dominated by cool wet weather from the Pacific Northwest. The abundance of rainfall makes the forests lush, green, dense, and damp. The park's western slopes, which catch most of the moisture coming from the west, are more lush than the east. The vagaries of elevation and weather combine to produce four distinctive life zones within the park: grassland and prairie; the Canadian zone, with massive lodgepole pine forests covering hundreds of square miles; the Hudsonian zone, a transition area with whitebark pine, alder, and other trees that are able to withstand long winters; and the Arctic-Alpine zone, with so-called *krummholz,* or "crooked-wood," forests of gnarled and dwarfed fir.

This unusually extensive range of topography supports a remarkable array of plants and wildlife. More than 1,000 plant species provide haven and food for 60 kinds of native animals and some 200 species of birds. Moose are the park's largest mammals. There also are white-tailed and mule deer, as well as elusive herds of elk and dozens of small mammals, such as badgers, rabbits, ground squirrels, pine martens, and coyotes. Mountain lions and rare northern Rocky Mountain gray wolves also have been spotted. A cousin of the smaller black bear, the grizzly, is the park's most famous resident. Considered endangered, about 600 grizzlies roam the park and nearby wilderness lands. Distinguished by a hump on its shoulders, the grizzly, generally eats grasses, berries, and roots, despite its reputation as an aggressive predator.

Glacier National Park

Established:	1910 (Waterton-Glacier International Peace Park was established 1932.)
Location:	Montana and Alberta, Canada
When to go:	Open all year. (Winter access is limited.)
Size:	Glacier: 1,013,572 acres; Waterton: 73,800 acres
Terrain:	Mountains, valleys, glaciers, lakes, forests, and prairie
Interesting sights:	Going-to-the-Sun Road and the Garden Wall
Wildlife:	Black and grizzly bear, moose, elk, deer, badger, rabbit, squirrel, coyote, mountain lion, and gray wolf
Activities:	Ranger-led walks, campfire programs, and slide shows; climbing, hiking, horseback riding, boating, fishing, bicycling, nature courses, cross-country skiing, and backpacking
Services:	Three visitor centers, seven park lodges and motels, and 13 campgrounds
Information:	West Glacier, Montana 59936; 406-888-5441

A bighorn ram, his horns curved backward in a graceful arc, surveys the world from a high rocky ledge that would be totally inaccessible for a less surefooted creature.

Opposite: *Closely crowded forests of tall Englemann spruce fill the valley, ringing the pristine waters of glacial Lake Josephine with cool shade.*

Mesa Verde
Palaces of Stone

This Anasazi bowl is easily recognized as having been made at Mesa Verde because of its distinctive geometric design in black on white.

Opposite: *Snuggled into a deep cave cut in soft sandstone, Cliff Palace is well-protected from the winter snows that fill the canyon and blanket the mesa.*

Right: *Spanish explorers could not have chosen a more appropriate name for this high, 15-mile-long tableland, shrouded in piñon and other dusty green desert plants, than Mesa Verde.*

G hosts haunt the cliffs and adobe dwellings of Mesa Verde. The Ancient Ones are long gone, but you can feel their spirits as you walk through these silent buildings that have stood for centuries in rock alcoves far above the ground. The structures are startlingly intact as if they are waiting for the return of their builders who left suddenly about seven hundred years ago. But the people who abandoned these buildings in such a livable state that many archaeologists believe they surely intended to return were not the first people to arrive here. Nearly 2,500 years ago, nomadic hunters and gathers wandered into what is now the southwestern corner of Colorado. There in the canyons and gullies of a high mesa they established what was to become an advanced culture that prospered for more than a millennium.

The first people of Mesa Verde, or green mesa, as it was called by Spanish explorers and priests who came through the area in the sixteenth century, lived in caves. Later they dug pit houses into the ground and covered them with logs and mud. These people were farmers, who grew corn and beans, and they became basket weavers of consummate skill. By about the eighth century A.D., they were building houses above ground with poles and mud. These apartment buildings, or pueblos, were built on the mesa's top and had as many as 50 rooms, usually arranged in the shape of a crescent. By now the people had given up baskets and begun making pottery, some of which still survives. Decorated with black and white geometric designs, these pots are remarkable for their exquisitely sensitive artistic expression.

This kiva at Step House once had a roof supported by masonry pilasters, but it is otherwise complete, with a stone bench ringing the wall and a masonry deflector to shield the fire pit.

• •

Around 1200 the mesa people moved down into recesses in the cliffs that formed the walls of canyons cut into the mesa. The reasons for the move are unknown today, but archaeologists speculate that the people may have been threatened by tribes of newcomers. There in the cliffs they built sturdy, compact apartment buildings with as many as four stories and 50 rooms. Many of the buildings had courtyards with kivas dug into them. These underground chambers, which are reminiscent of their ancestors' first dwellings on the mesa's top, were used for religious ceremonies. Although their culture was surprisingly advanced, with complex trade networks supplying such goods as turquoise and shells from as far away as the Pacific Coast, life was harsh for the people of the cliff dwellings, and few lived beyond the age of 35.

In the thirteenth century, the cliff-dwelling people began to leave their homes. By the end of the century, all of them were gone, never to return. Why did they go? At the turn of this century, archaeologists thought enemies had arrived,

but there is no evidence of warfare. Today archaeologists believe that the Anasazi's very successes on the mesa may have turned against them. Their dryland farming was so productive, archaeologists think, that the population may have grown too swiftly, reaching as many as 5,000 people on Mesa Verde alone. Gradually this huge population began taking its toll on the environment: Game was hunted out, the soil was depleted, and the woodlands were cut away. Years of drought and poor crops may have been the final blow.

Two cowboys discovered the ruins in 1888. Tracking wandering cattle through a snowstorm on top of the mesa, they stopped on the edge of a steep canyon. Through the snow they could see the faint outline of the walls and towers of what looked like a huge palace of stone on the far side of the canyon. Excited, they made a ladder and climbed down to the deserted cliff city and explored its ghostly network of deserted rooms. Inside they found such artifacts as tools and pottery. Their condition was so good

Long House, a fortress on Wetherill Mesa, rivals Cliff House in its scope and grandeur. It was opened to park visitors in 1972 after extensive archeological study.

that some of the items were still usable. They named the dwelling Cliff Palace, and archaeologists later determined that no one had stood in the rooms explored by the cowboys for nearly six centuries.

Today Mesa Verde National Park encompasses more than 4,000 prehistoric sites that were used by the people the Navajo call the Anasazi, which means something approximating "Ancient Ones." The structures and ruins include mesa-top pit houses and pueblos, as well as the ghostly multistoried cliff villages for which the park is famous.

Because of the dry climate, the cliff dwellings are in a nearly unbelievable state of preservation. They are located in sandstone canyons that slice the mesa into narrow tablelands. The Anasazi built these dwellings in natural alcoves formed by water that had percolated down through the sandstone. When seeping water reached a denser layer of shale, it flowed horizontally through the canyon wall, eroding the cliff into deep, rounded shelters. Several of the major cliff ruins are open to visitors who reach them by trails, walkways, and steps that lead down from the mesa top. The silent stone and the mystery of the Anasazi create an experience most people never forget. Novelist Willa Cather experienced the ruins as "more like sculpture than anything else."

Exploring Spruce Tree House

Spruce Tree House, Mesa Verde's best preserved ruin, is a fine example of Anasazi construction techniques and skillful stonework. Today you can reach the site by a short paved trail that crosses the canyon floor through a stand of Gambel oak trees. The nuts of the trees were eaten by the Anasazi. Believed to have housed more than 100 people, the dwelling is about 200 feet long and contains eight kivas. Three of them have reconstructed roofs, and you can climb into one of the kivas through a smoke hole to get a sense of what the dark chamber might have been like during an ancient religious ritual.

The dwelling was named by early explorers who climbed down a tall tree to reach it. The tree is a Douglas fir, but they thought it was a spruce. Other equally remarkable and ghostly cliff dwellings in the park include Cliff Palace, the first discovered and largest pre-Columbian dwelling in North America, and Balcony House. Perched high up in a cliff alcove, Balcony House was easily defended. Visitors to this site face the adventure of climbing up a 32-foot ladder and crawling through a tunnel on their hands and knees.

Mesa Verde National Park

Established:	1906
Location:	Colorado
When to go:	Open all year. (Winter access is limited.)
Size:	52,085 acres
Terrain:	Mesa, canyons, and gullies
Interesting sights:	Spruce Tree House and Cliff Palace
Wildlife:	Rabbit, mule deer, lizards, small mammals, and birds.
Activities:	Ranger-led archaeological walks, cliff dwellings tours, and campfire programs; way-side exhibits, self-guided tours, limited hiking on two trails (backpacking is not permitted in park), cross-country skiing, and snowshoeing
Services:	Visitor center, museum, park lodge, and one campground
Information:	Mesa Verde National Park, Colorado 81330; 303-529-4465

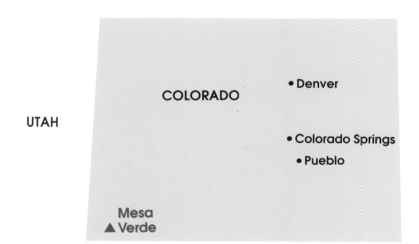

UTAH

COLORADO

• Denver

• Colorado Springs

• Pueblo

Mesa
▲ Verde

NEW MEXICO

ARIZONA

Spruce Tree House is the best preserved and one of the largest cliff dwellings, with 114 rooms and eight kivas. Its high walls still touch the roof of the cave.

Big Bend
Rio Grande Country

Mariscal is one of three great canyons in the park. (Boquilllas and Santa Elena are the others.) Before the Rio Grande was dammed, Mariscal boasted some of the whitest white water in America.

Opposite: At sunrise a pale moon sets over the Chisos Mountains, while the first light of morning turns the Rio Grande into a silvery path through the desert.

Right: Winter seems out of place in a desert park like Big Bend, but January usually dusts the Chisos Mountains with light snow.

In the sixteenth century, Spanish explorers traipsed through the valley of the Rio Grande in what is now southern Texas. According to legend, they discovered a rich lode of silver at the top of a jagged mountain near a bend in the river where it had cut a spectacularly deep canyon. The Spanish soldiers enslaved the native people to work the mine, but eventually the miners rebelled, killed their Spanish overlords, and sealed the entrance to the mine so they would never have to work there again.

Looking like an ancient abandoned castle atop a hill, Lost Mine Peak is today a landmark of Big Bend National Park, which encompasses an immense expanse of dry mountains, canyons, and desert wilderness just across the Rio Grande from Mexicò. Here the river winds south, then suddenly veers north in a great horseshoe curve before turning southward again. The region within the great triangle, an area as large as Massachusetts and Connecticut combined, is known as Big Bend country. Forming the southern border of the park, the Rio Grande has sliced a deep chasm, called Santa Elena Canyon, through red and orange rock. The canyon is so deep and narrow in places that the sun barely penetrates it.

This is a wild land with a wild history. People arrived in Big Bend country about 10,000 years ago. They were probably nomadic tribes whose ancestors had recently crossed the Bering land bridge from Asia. The first farmers began cultivating the rich bottomland near the river in the thirteenth century A.D. These people may have wandered into the valley from Pueblo cities to the north. When Spanish soldiers and settlers arrived in the sixteenth century, they captured the indigenous people and sold them as slaves. Soon more warlike tribes, such as the

Mescalero Apaches, moved in from the north, launching lightning attacks on the Spanish settlements. Later the Comanches made their way into the region, driven by encroaching white settlers from the Comancheria, their prairie homeland in northwest Texas. Skilled horse fighters, the Comanche warriors victimized both Spanish ranchers and Apaches, killing, taking slaves to sell in Mexico, and destroying livestock and crops. They eventually drove the Spanish settlers from the region. In 1821 Big Bend country became part of Mexico, and 15 years later, part of the Republic of Texas.

Today Big Bend remains a special place; it is at once desolate, haunting, and fascinating. Within the park are archaeological treasures, petrified trees, vestiges of prehistoric cultures, and unusual forms of plant and animal life. Geologically, the park encompasses some of the most fascinating and complex landforms on earth. Hundreds of millions of years ago, first one and then another great inland sea flowed through the region, depositing thick layers of limestone and fossil-bearing shale. About 60 million years ago, mountains began thrusting up. At about the same time, a 40-mile-wide plain began sinking along fault lines. This left the awesome cliffs of Santa Elena Canyon to the west and the Sierra del Carmen mountains to the east that rise about 1,500 feet above the desert. About 35 million years ago, volcanic activity began spewing vast amounts of ash and dust into the air and squeezing out magma, or molten rock, to form the Chisos Mountains. Some of the magma that cooled and hardened underground was later exposed by erosion, leaving the park's striking landscape. Today the Chisos are a cool, moist island with temperatures that can be 20 degrees cooler than the surrounding desert.

Early on a winter morning, the Grapevine Hills are an excellent place to watch for swift mule deer and tough-skinned javelina.

Exploring Big Bend

T he Chisos are mountains of legend. Look closely at Pulliam Bluff in Chisos Basin, and you might see the profile of a reclining man's face. According to legend, this is Alsate, a mighty Apache chief, whose ghost still roams the higher mountains. His campfire can still be seen at night, it is said.

The mountains are ideal for hiking, and many of the choicest hikes begin from the trailhead in Chisos Basin. One of these, a short stroll up Window View Trail, reveals a photogenic formation called the Window, a deep V-shaped opening through which water drains from the basin. This spot is especially lovely at sunset when vivid colors streak the sky and long shadows add mystery to the landforms.

Visitors can also walk to the Window for a spectacular view of a mountain called Casa Grande, or "big house." Dawn and dusk add to the spectacle of this especially stunning vista. On the South Rim, you will find a fine oasis of bigtooth maple, Douglas fir, and Arizona pine. This is the yellow Colima warbler's only home in the United States.

Visitors to Big Bend imagine that they see all kinds of shapes in the stately contours of the Chisos Mountains, but the rectangular profile of Casa Grande is unmistakable.

The 1,500-foot sheer limestone cliffs of Santa Elena Canyon hold the mighty Rio Grande to a narrow channel and allow sunlight to penetrate their depths only briefly each morning.

Life in Big Bend

The remarkable topographic variety within Big Bend provides a habitat for a surprising diversity of life. Here there are 1,000 plant species, many found nowhere else on earth, and more than 400 species of birds, which is many more kinds of birds than you will find in any other national park. Desert vegetation covers most of the park's terrain; bunchgrasses, cactus, creosote bushes, yuccas, and sotols grow in vast profusion. Sotols are bright green plants with sawtooth edges on their leaves, and the Apaches used to roast and eat the sotol. Fermenting it yields an alcoholic drink.

A heavy spring rain can momentarily transform the desert. Normally dry creek beds rage with water, and dormant seeds create short-lived fields of wildflowers. Elsewhere in the park, the Rio Grande, with its deep canyons and floodplains, creates an ecosystem all its own, as do the cool Chisos Mountains, which harbor forests of pine and oak that provide a habitat for deer, mountain lions, and other animals.

Big Bend National Park

Established:	1944
Location:	Texas
When to go:	Open all year. (Fall and winter are the best seasons.)
Size:	802,541 acres
Terrain:	Canyons, mountains, river, and desert
Interesting sights:	The Window and Casa Grande
Wildlife:	Deer, mountain lion, javelina, and hundreds of bird species
Activities:	Ranger-led nature walks, raft trips, and evening programs; hiking, fishing, river rafting, horseback riding, nature seminars, and backpacking
Services:	Two visitor centers, information stations, park lodge, four campgrounds, and a trailer park
Information:	Big Bend National Park, Texas 79834; 915-477-2251

The Rio Grande flows through the desert bringing life to the parched landscape. This ribbonlike oasis allows beavers, crayfish, heron, and an abundance of fish to survive in an otherwise extremely hostile environment.

Opposite: *The Chihuahuan Desert is a place of intense heat, scarce water, and wide-open spaces, but it is also graced with a stunning array of animals and plants, including yucca, sotol, prickly pear, and sagebrush.*

Guadalupe Mountains
History in the Desert

El Capitan and Guadalupe Peak are the highest parts of an oval-shaped fossil reef, most of which lies buried beneath the desert in West Texas and southern New Mexico.

Opposite: *From as far away as 50 miles, El Capitan can be seen rising almost straight up out of the flat, desolate wasteland that surrounds it.*

Right: *Looking out across barren salt flats toward the Guadalupe Mountains, it is difficult to image that their highest elevations are decidedly alpine in character.*

The dry flatlands of the Chihuahuan Desert, a vast, barren stretch of cactus and greasewood that extends for hundreds of miles across West Texas and south into Mexico, seem an unlikely place to find an ocean reef. But here hundreds of miles from the nearest saltwater, an immense escarpment of orange and red limestone that was once on the bottom of a sea glistens in the bright sunlight. The Guadalupe Mountains, a V-shaped range with its northern arm extending into New Mexico and its southern arm pointing toward Mexico, rise more than a mile above the desert. Visible for nearly 50 miles, a great monolithic rock called El Capitan, which in Spanish means "the chief," rises audaciously at the point of the V. For centuries it has been a landmark for travelers crossing this vast desert.

At more than a mile and a half above sea level, El Capitan (8,085 feet) and adjacent Guadalupe Peak (8,751 feet) are the two tallest mountains in Texas. The peaks are the most obvious sections of the Capitan Reef, most of which still lies buried thousands of feet below the desert's surface. More than 200 million years ago, the immense reef enclosed about 10,000 square miles of a shallow inland sea. The reef was formed as the remains of lime-secreting algae and other primitive creatures that lived in the sea washed ashore. Gradually the climate of the region changed, and the sea dried up, leaving much of the reef exposed. More millennia passed, and the seabed and the reef were buried beneath a vast plain, where they remained for millions of years. Then, about 12 million years ago, geologic processes deep beneath the earth raised and tilted the ancient seabed and reef, leaving the 40-mile section now known as the Guadalupe Mountains high and dry. In the process the reef was fractured in several places. Over more millions of years, wind

and water worked to turn these deep cracks into lovely canyons that slice into the mountains we see today. These chasms, including McKittrick Canyon, Dog Canyon, and many others, are the heart of Guadalupe Mountains National Park.

Archaeological remnants, such as spear tips, knife blades, bits of basket work, and pottery shards, attest to a human presence in the Guadalupe Mountains that goes back about 12,000 years. When people first came to the area, during the decline of the last Pleistocene ice age, the climate was wet and humid. The first people who lived here probably foraged for food and hunted such animals as camels and mammoths. By the time Spanish explorers appeared in about 1550, wandering Mescalero Apaches often made their camps at springs near the base of the range. Apache and Spanish legends about great treasures of gold and silver hidden in the mountains eventually drew American prospectors to this desert. In the years after the Civil War, they were followed by farmers, ranchers, and the U.S. Cavalry. In the Guadalupe Mountains, the Mescalero Apaches made their last stand, but by 1890 virtually every Apache had been killed or forced onto a reservation. Initially the territory was taken over by private ranching and mining interests. Over time enough land was donated to create a park, which is still being expanded as more land becomes available to the park service.

Exploring Guadalupe Mountains

The special wonders of this national park are found in the steep contoured canyons that cut deeply into the Guadalupe Mountains. The canyons hold forested glens of deciduous trees and alligator juniper alongside meadows of hip-high grasses and creosote plants. In Dog Canyon, among stands of Gambel oak, Douglas fir, and limber pine, you can still see Apache mescal-roasting pits.

Five miles long and thousands of feet deep, McKittrick Canyon contains an array of life and geological history unique to our planet. Amid forests of oak, juniper, maple, and the lovely Texas madrone with its oddly twisted red bark, you can find the remnants of the floor of a sea that covered the area more than 200 million years ago. Above you, inlaid in the canyon walls, are millions of years of geological history told by layers of ancient fossils and startling rock formations. The canyon was named for Kid McKittrick, a bank robber. Legend says he hid in the canyon after fleeing from New Mexico. He was never captured, and he supposedly left a cache of loot buried somewhere in the canyon.

Guadalupe Mountains National Park

Established:	1972
Location:	Texas
When to go:	Open all year
Size:	86,416 acres
Terrain:	Mountains, canyons, and desert
Interesting sights:	El Capitan and McKittrick Canyon
Wildlife:	Mountain lion, javelina, rattlesnake, fox, ground squirrel, skunk, raccoon, other small mammals, birds, and reptiles
Activities:	Ranger-led walks and talks; hiking, horseback trail riding, and backpacking
Services:	Two visitor centers, a ranger station, and two campgrounds
Information:	HC 60, Box 400, Salt Flat, Texas 79847; 915-828-3251

In autumn McKittrick Canyon comes alive when the bright seasonal hues of oak, maple, and cottonwood contrast with the dense green of towering pines and the sparkle of spring-fed streams.

Carlsbad Caverns

Sculpture Beneath the Desert

· ·

If you have trouble remembering which cave formations are stalactites and which are stalagmites, just remember that stalactites "stick tight" to the cave's ceiling.

Opposite: *Large cave features form when there is a plentiful water supply above the cave, but these relatively new, slender stalactites are the result of desertlike conditions on the surface.*

Right: *Each night a cloud of 250,000 bats flies out of the gaping natural entrance to Carlsbad Caverns and spreads out across the desert in search of flying insects.*

At sunset on summer evenings, in a corner of the Guadalupe Mountains in southern New Mexico, a dark cloud swirls out of the ground, a tornado of a half million bats flying out of an immense opening in the earth. The bats fan out over an area 100 miles wide, catching and devouring tons of flying insects. At dawn they return to their home. This nightly exodus of Mexican free-tailed bats led to the modern rediscovery of Carlsbad Caverns in about 1900. This great cave is one of the largest caverns in the world. The size and boldness of its huge vaulted underground chambers are truly awesome. The cave contains formations of such startling shapes and colors, and of such monumental proportions that cowboy humorist Will Rogers once called this underground wonderland "the Grand Canyon with a roof on it."

People have known about these spectacular caverns for thousands of years. According to archaeological evidence, nomadic hunters and gatherers used the cave's enormous mouth for shelter. Apparently, they did not penetrate far inside. Shortly after its turn-of-the-century rediscovery, miners began excavating the cave for its huge deposits of bat guano, which was shipped to southern California for use as a fertilizer in citrus groves. One miner, a young man from the area named James Larkin White, was so intrigued by the cave that he undertook a serious exploration of the labyrinthine caverns beyond Bat Cave. His passionate interest in the cave garnered the publicity

· ·

that helped establish Carlsbad Caverns as a national monument in 1923 and a national park seven years later. White served as its chief ranger.

The full extent of the caverns has still not been fully explored. To date 20 miles have been investigated and mapped. Three of the most spectacular miles, which contain the great vaulted chambers, King's Palace, Queen's Chamber, and Green Lake Room, are open to park visitors. Throughout the caverns there is a profusion of multicolored rock formations, such as the Iceberg, Bone Yard, and Rock of Ages, that owe their startling hues to iron oxide deposits in the rock about the cave.

The same reef that forms the Guadalupe Mountains also spawned Carlsbad Caverns. Over time, fractures in the ancient limestone sedimentation appeared, allowing seeping, mineral-laden water to cut through the rock and form the caverns. The cave's stunning interior decoration is also the work of limestone-carrying water. Over the millennia dripping water has built a nearly unbelievable array of formations: some are six stories tall; others are as delicate as lace.

The Big Room

When you ride an elevator into the depths of Carlsbad Caverns or walk down well-made trails into the cave, remember that the first visitors descended into the caverns in guano buckets lowered by pulleys. Tours used to begin in the uppermost of the cave's three largest chambers, the Bat Cave, but this area is now closed to everyone except the bats. At a level 750 feet below the surface, the Hall of the Giants contains the cavern's biggest stalagmites, the Rock of Ages, Giant Dome, and Twin Domes. These monster monoliths seem to be straining toward the great vaulted ceiling hundreds of feet above them. On this level you can also tour the Boneyard, which is filled with structures that only slightly resemble bones, and Iceberg Rock, a 100,000 ton hunk of stone. But everything else within the caverns is dwarfed by the Big Room, the largest known underground chamber in the Western Hemisphere. This immense enclosure is 1,800 feet long and up to 1,100 feet wide. It is so vast that it could contain more than a dozen football fields, and it is so tall that you could build a 30-story building inside.

At the 830-foot level are other large rooms, the King's Palace with statuesque stalagmites and the lovely Queen's Chamber with rock that seems to flow like draperies. The park service used to affix names to the cavern's rock formations, but recently rangers have removed most of the name labels. Now you can let your imagination work its own wonders. What do you think these weird and improbable formations resemble? A ship? A wedding cake? A Japanese garden?

Carlsbad Caverns National Park

Established:	1930
Location:	New Mexico
When to go:	Open all year, except Christmas Day
Size:	46,755 acres
Terrain:	Desert mountains and cavern
Interesting sights:	The Rock of Ages and the Big Room
Wildlife:	Mexican free-tailed bat, ground squirrel, skunk, raccoon, fox, desert reptiles, and golden eagle
Activities:	Ranger-led cavern tours; self-guided audio tours, dusk bat flight program, desert nature trail, hiking, backpacking, and picnicking
Services:	Visitor center and backcountry camping
Information:	3225 National Parks Highway, Carlsbad, New Mexico 88220; 505-785-2232

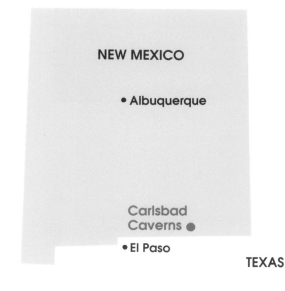

The Rock of Ages is one of several of Carlsbad's largest stalagmites located in the Hall of Giants on the 750-foot level of the cave.

Arches
Windows on the Deser.

· ·

The Fiery Furnace in Arches is a labyrinth of salmon-colored Entrada sandstone fins. The snow-capped La Sal Mountains are about 20 miles southeast of the park.

Opposite: *Landscape Arch defies the laws of engineering. It is 291 feet long, 65 feet high, and only six feet thick at its narrowest point and getting thinner.*

Right: *Devil's Garden Trail is located at the northern end of the scenic drive through Arches. Its two miles of easy walking convey visitors through a breathtaking natural sculpture garden.*

Chiseled by the powerful forces of wind and water, this surprising natural rock garden contains the planet's most remarkable collections of abstract sculpture. Arches National Park sits on a great plateau in southeastern Utah, encompassing a stark landscape of broken red sandstone. The park contains more than 950 natural stone arches. But these spectacular sandstone portals, braced against the desert sky and revealing startlingly lovely desert terrain through their openings, are only part of Arches' stunning landscape.

A fantasyland in rock, the park is filled with giant balanced rocks that look as though they are about to teeter and fall. There are pedestals and spires that resemble a child's drip castles expanded to enormous scale. Glistening slickrock domes are inlaid with swirls of stone cut by red sandy washes and dotted with wildflowers in spring. These formations sparkle and shimmer beneath an enormous blue sky.

Arches is perched atop the Colorado Plateau, a high desert region stretching from western Colorado across southern Utah and northern New Mexico to Arizona. This area is the most sparsely populated region in the southern 48 states, but it contains the nation's greatest wealth of national parks. It is a place teeming with scenic treasures almost beyond belief: mountains, gorges, rushing rivers, great canyons, escarpments, buttes, spires, pinnacles, and endless stretches of starkly lovely desert landscape.

High above the Colorado River, Arches National Park is a geological maelstrom that has been shaped by aeon after aeon of weathering by rain, snow, ice, and wind. Most of the

· ·

formations in the park are composed of Entrada sandstone, which geologists say was part of a low arid coastal plain adjacent to a great inland sea 150 to 200 million years ago. Over time the sand was covered by layers of sediment and hardened into rock. Then the land was lifted up, tilted, and eroded until the Entrada layer was exposed to the weather. At first water and wind cracked the exposed sandstone. Then narrow canyons and gullies were scoured out of the stone, leaving thin walls called fins in between.

The final phase in the process, or at least final as we see it today, occurred as wind and frost brushed away at the soft interior area of some of these fins, eventually perforating them with a window. This gradually enlarged until the window became an arch. The park's most photographed attraction, Delicate Arch, is isolated in its own amphitheater and frames a stunning view of endless sandstone. Landscape Arch, with a span of nearly 300 feet, is the longest known natural bridge in the world and one of seven arches along the two-mile-long Devils Garden Trail.

Arches Scenic Drive

Arches National Park is more than a concentration of spectacular rock arches. Well-preserved petroglyphs carved into a cliff in the park testify that people have inhabited the region for a long time. The pictures depict riders on horseback, indicating that the carvings were made sometime after the middle of the sixteenth century when Spanish explorers first introduced horses to the Southwest. These petroglyphs increase our sense of the timelessness of this place. We know that the landscape here is constantly changing. Such natural spectacles as the Fiery Furnace, a dense array of red fins, could one day become arches. But today we admire them as they appear to turn into tongues of fire when the sun is low in the sky.

The scenic drive through Arches climbs from the floor of Moab Canyon to Devils Garden. Along this 18-mile one-way drive, you pass a lovely slickrock expanse called the Petrified Dunes; these ancient sand dunes have hardened into stone. With the snowcapped La Sal Mountains rising in the distance, the dunes are a spectacle of form and contrast. Other sights are equally spectacular: Balanced Rock, a striking, eroded stone spire 128 feet high; South Window Arch, 105 feet wide; and the dramatic Double Arch.

Arches National Park

Established:	1971
Location:	Utah
When to go:	Open all year. (The best seasons are spring and fall.)
Size:	77,739 acres
Terrain:	High desert plateau with unusual rock formations
Interesting sights:	Delicate Arch and Fiery Furnace
Wildlife:	Small desert mammals, reptiles, and birds
Activities:	Ranger-led walks and evening programs; self-guided auto tour, hiking, float and powerboat trips, jeep tours, horseback riding, and backpacking
Services:	Visitor center and one campground
Information:	P.O. Box 907, Moab, Utah 84532; 801-259-8161

• Salt Lake City

COLORADO
• Grand Junction

Arches
▲
Moab •

UTAH

Balanced Rock looks precarious, but geologists estimate that it has taken nature 60 million years to create this masterpiece and expect it will take millions more years to erode the spire and topple the rock.

Delicate Arch, which is 65 feet tall and 35 feet wide, perches precariously on the rim of a canyon. The arch is all that remains of a sandstone wall, or fin.

Capitol Reef
The Land Rose Up

Access to Cathedral Valley is limited to four-wheel-drive vehicles, but the spectacular red sandstone monoliths collected here are well worth the adventurous trip.

Opposite: *The park is named for this rock outcropping, capped with white sandstone, that reminded the early pioneers of the capitol dome in Washington, D.C.*

Right: *The same natural forces that wore away Entrada sandstone to form the arches in Canyonlands and Arches shaped Hickman Bridge, one of two arches in Capitol Reef.*

From a distance it looks like a swell of gigantic ocean waves, but the Waterpocket Fold, of which Capitol Reef is a part, is an immense pleat in the earth's crust that rises in great parallel ridges for 100 miles across the starkly beautiful desert landscape of southern Utah. The awe-inspiring formation is not actually a reef, which is a ridge of limestone that once existed in an ocean. But Waterpocket Fold is one of the world's largest and finest monoclinal flexures. In these unusual places, the earth's crust has buckled upwards. The early pioneers, who were not geologists, called any rocky barrier to their travel a reef, and this reef's sheer cliffs, which are nearly 1,000 feet high in some places, blocked east-west travel in this region for decades.

Over the centuries the exposed edges of the uplift have eroded into a slickrock wilderness that encompasses most of the park's scenic splendors. Layer upon layer of brightly colored sandstone is cut by deep, serpentine canyons or eroded into natural bridges or massive domes. One of these great monolithic rock structures apparently reminded an early traveler of the capitol dome, and he came up with the name Capitol Reef.

The park is in such a remote corner of the Colorado Plateau that the nearest traffic light is about 80 miles away. But for centuries Capitol Reef has been known as a place of dramatic beauty that has drawn visitors to gaze at its wonders or reap its bounty. Ancient petroglyphs, often figures of bighorn sheep and other animals, were cut into rock walls by people who inhabited this area more than 700 years ago. The people who carved these figures once plowed fields in the central area of today's park where towering cliffs contrast with a green oasis along the Fremont River.

In the nineteenth century, Mormon pioneers farmed and planted orchards in the valley leaving behind the apple, peach, and apricot trees that are still there. The last residents left in the early 1960s, but cattle drives through the park still bring back the feeling of the frontier days. In the southern end of the park, wonderful wilderness trails wind through places with such poetic names as Muley Twist Canyon. This path is so narrow that in pioneer days mules had to slither through the canyon. Elsewhere the pioneers descriptively dubbed the terrain Poverty Flat, Fern's Nipple, Tarantula Mesa, and Dogwater Creek. To the north the lovely Cathedral Valley reveals eroded spires of Entrada sandstone that rise 50 stories from the valley floor. In Cathedral Valley a narrow four-wheel-drive road loops among stark and bizarre formations with such names as the Gypsum Sinkhole, the Walls of Jericho, and the Temple of the Sun.

Sometimes lucky park visitors encounter a herd of desert bighorn sheep. The last sighting of a native bighorn was in 1948, and park officials believe that they disappeared because of diseases caught from domestic sheep. The park introduced the desert bighorn in 1984.

In 1869, on his way down the Colorado River, John Wesley Powell encountered the Dirty Devil River, which he later, less descriptively, renamed the Fremont River.

Capitol Reef Scenic Drive

Capitol Reef's lovely, 25-mile-long scenic drive leads into the heart of the park along an old wagon trail, called the Blue Dugway. Legend has it that this road has been used by Native Americans, outlaws, miners, and gypsies. It is said that the Devil himself was once spotted strolling on the trail. A pioneer farmer supposedly drove him away with the Book of Mormon. Today the Blue Dugway is graded and covered. It leads from the former Mormon community of Fruita along the section of the Waterpocket Fold called Capitol Reef.

One spur road leads into the Grand Wash, a canyon supposedly used as a hideout by the famous outlaw Butch Cassidy. From the trailhead in the canyon, a spectacular hiking trail leads down to the Fremont River through a series of narrows, while another trail climbs for a mile up to an imposing rock formation known as Cassidy Arch.

Capitol Reef National Park

Established:	1971
Location:	Utah
When to go:	Open all year
Size:	241,904 acres
Terrain:	High desert ridges, canyons, and river valley
Interesting sights:	Muley Twist Canyon and Cassidy Arch
Wildlife:	Desert bighorn sheep, mule deer, small mammals, reptiles, and birds
Activities:	Ranger-led nature walks and evening programs; interpretive exhibits, scenic drives, hiking, fruit picking, birdwatching, horseback trips, jeep tours, and backpacking (by permit)
Services:	Visitor center and three campgrounds
Information:	Torrey, Utah 84775; 801-425-3791

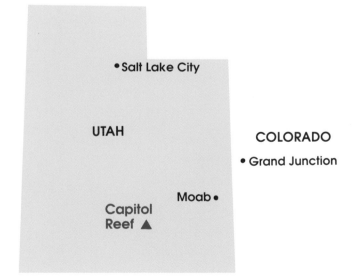

Capitol Reef is part of a 100-mile-long bulge in the earth's surface, known as the Waterpocket Fold, which catches gallons of water in its eroded pockets after each rainfall.

Canyonlands
Geological Wonderland

Elephant Canyon was shaped by a unique combination of geologic events and the powerful forces of water, frost, and gravity.

Opposite: *From Grand View Point, a vast panorama of more than 2,500 square miles of rocks and canyons stretches out toward the horizon.*

Right: *Viewed from Dead Horse Point above Gooseneck Meander, the winding Colorado River flows proudly through the deep canyon it has created.*

Canyonlands encompasses a vast sandstone wilderness cut by great chasms and gorges. From all appearances this is one of the most arid places on earth, but this place was forged by water surging through the terrain in two unusually abrasive rivers. Their combined energy has created what is surely one of the most spectacular examples of the power of erosion by water anywhere on earth. This is a landscape of deep shadowed canyons, bright orange mesas, great buff-colored pinnacles, and maroon buttes—an intense pallet of natural colors that comes alive in the rays of the setting sun.

The terrain here seems so surreal that it looks as though it might have been painted by Salvador Dali. The landscape seems to be in the midst of either its birth pangs or its death throes. The wild array of arches, sandstone pillars and needles, canyon mazes, and scarps that make up the otherworldly terrain of Canyonlands National Park is the work of the Colorado and Green rivers. They meet in the heart of the park at a spectacular site, called the Confluence. The rivers form a great Y cut 1,000 feet into the brilliantly hued sandstone. From the Confluence the rivers roll on as one. Over the 20 million years of its existence, the combined Colorado River has carried away solid rock from an area the size of Texas and two miles deep. The abrasive power of this sediment, helped by wind, precipitation, and frost, has carved out deep canyons, stark mesas, and high buttes unlike any seen elsewhere on earth. The remarkable stripes that run through the nearly unbelievable shapes of these figures are the result of the way in which different kinds of stone have resisted the constant aggression of these natural sculpting agents. The perpendicular landscape of the region was also shaped by underlying deposits of salt. Under great pressure from the rock

The Needles began as rectangular blocks of Cedar Mesa sandstone. Over time erosion widened the gaps between the blocks, creating slender spires and hoodoos.

above, the salt is formed into huge domes that eventually fracture the surface.

The two rivers that flow together in the park divide it into three sections. In the north a high mesa, called the Island in the Sky, rises as a great scarp 2,000 feet above the Confluence. In the east is the district known as the Needles. Here giant pinnacles banded with alternating white and red stone rise 400 feet above the grassy floors of valleys ringed by perpendicular cliffs. Across the conjunction of the rivers to the west lies the Maze, an isolated wedge of canyon country. At the end of a 14-mile trail, the Maze Overlook offers a spectacular vista of rivers, spires, clefts, and canyons. Many people argue that this is the finest view in the Southwest.

Canyonlands is mostly wilderness, with paved highways penetrating only its periphery. Trails and jeep roads lead into some of its most scenic and geologically flamboyant places. They meander along the rims of high plateaus, then plunge dramatically down steep canyon walls where the descent or ascent can be as great as 40 percent. As you drop into Canyonlands, the ground falls away from you in giant stair steps; flat benchlands end abruptly in rock walls. The eerie look of a landscape so wild and the terrain so treacherous caused writer Edward Abbey to describe Canyonlands as the "most arid, most hostile, most lonesome, most grim bleak barren desolate and savage quarter of the state of Utah—the best part by far."

The Needles

Visitors without a four-wheel-drive vehicle can get a real feel for Canyonlands by driving into the Needles area on the eastern side of the park. Here is a spectacular landscape of deep canyons, unusual flat-bottomed valleys, called grabens; sandstone formations, such as the descriptively named Molar Rock; and numerous arches. An 18-mile-long paved road, with dirt spurs, leads into the area. It begins at Squaw Flat, a grassy area with piñon pine trees and junipers. At Pothole Point you can walk to rock depressions that fill with rain water. These little lakes are an important source of water in canyon country. They often teem with life, such as snails, fairy shrimp, and worms, which live through the dry summer months wrapped like mummies in dried mud.

From Pothole Point you follow the road to its destination at Big Spring Canyon. Here squat pedestals of sandstone rise like mushrooms from the barren bedrock. This point is the beginning of the trail that leads to Confluence Overlook, one of the most spectacular trails in the Southwest. The trail climbs the side of a canyon by means of a ladder, ending at a site more than 900 feet above the point where the rivers merge.

The Island in the Sky ascends from the bottom of the river's canyon in two giant steps: The first is a shelf of White Rim sandstone 4,000 feet high; the top is more than 6,000 feet high.

132

Canyonlands Pictographs

Canyonlands' pictographs (paintings on stone walls) lie in a detached section of the park, called the Hórseshoe Canyon Unit. At Ghost Gallery ancient figures painted in red ocher stare at you through the centuries with hollow eyes. Archaeologists believe that these life-size pictographs may be 6,000 years old. They do not look like the work of the Anasazi or any of the other people known to have lived in this region, so archaeologists surmise that the pictographs were left by earlier people. But nobody knows for sure.

More recent inhabitants of Canyonlands have also left behind reminders of their presence. These people were related to the Anasazi of Mesa Verde in Colorado and Chaco Canyon, a vast pueblo in western New Mexico. In Canyonlands they farmed and gathered plants. In the Needles area, you can still see a small but well-preserved granary used to store corn 700 years ago.

· ·

Canyonlands National Park

Established:	1964
Location:	Utah
When to go:	Open all year (Best seasons are spring and fall.)
Size:	337,570 acres
Terrain:	Desert canyonland, buttes, mesas, and rivers
Interesting sights:	The Needles and Horseshoe Canyon pictographs
Wildlife:	Small desert mammals and reptiles
Activities:	Ranger-led walks and talks; hiking, boating, rafting, bicycling, horseback riding, fishing, four-wheel-drive tours, river-running trips, and backpacking (by permit)
Services:	Four visitor centers and two campgrounds
Information:	125 W. 200 South, Moab, Utah 84532; 801-259-7164

This red-white-and-blue stylized human figure is known as All-American Man. The pictograph in the Needles District, along upper Salt Creek Canyon, is probably older than nearby Anasazi ruins.

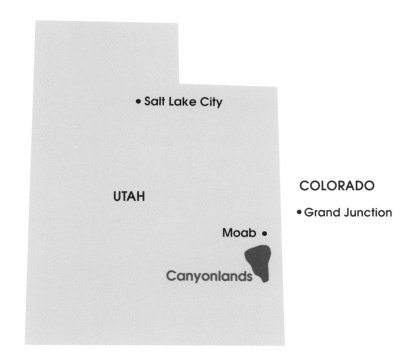

The opening in Angel Arch in Salt Creek Canyon is an exhilarating 160 feet high, but its name doesn't refer to a celestial portal. Someone thought the arch looked like a winged angel leaning against a harp.

Bryce Canyon
Palaces in Wonderland

· · · · · · · · · · · · ·

Natural Bridge, which is 96 feet high, has never straddled a river. It was hollowed out by the powerful forces of wind, rain, and ice.

Opposite: *Nature has filled the eroded bowl of Bryce Amphitheater with a host of delicate limestone pinnacles, spires, and fins.*

Right: *Visitors to Bryce never forget the unique intensity of light reflected by dazzling red sandstone against the bright blue sky, when it is focused through windows in the rock.*

The landscape is totally outlandish at Bryce Canyon. This is a place that looks like it has been gouged out of the earth, then filled with orange and red rock pedestals so fancifully and bizarrely formed that they look like the inhabitants of a dreamworld. Called hoodoos, these endless rock towers are all shaped like something or someone you've seen in some other place: castles, bridges, towers, presidents, prime ministers, and even Queen Victoria. In fact everything looks like something else, so the questionable practice of affixing names to geological formations is forgivable here.

Bryce Canyon is the scalloped edge of a huge mesa and not a true canyon. It is a series of great amphitheaters eroded out of the Paunsaugunt Plateau in southwestern Utah. If you want to think of it as a canyon, you could think of it as half a canyon. On a grand scale the geological formation containing Bryce resembles a loaf of bread that has been chewed away on one side. Erosion has taken about a dozen big bites out of the pink cliffs that form the plateau's eastern rim. The Bryce escarpment, with its thousands of geological gargoyles and castellated spires, is the product of the relentless destructive powers of water and time. Under the onslaught of weather, nothing at Bryce remains the same for long, and the canyon is one of the best places on the planet to observe the forces that shape the surface of the earth.

A single summer cloudburst can carry off thousands of tons of gravel, sand, and silt to the Paria River and then on to the

· ·

Colorado River and into the Grand Canyon. Bryce is changing at a fantastic rate: Its rim is receding one foot every 65 years. The place is an open textbook of geology. Sixty million years ago, a vast body of water, called Lake Flagstaff, covered what is now southwestern Utah. As the ages passed, sediments of gravel, sand, and mud accumulated to thicknesses of 2,000 feet or more beneath the sea. Eventually cemented together by minerals and pressure, the sediments turned into solid rock, which is now called the Wasatch Formation.

Beginning about 16 million years ago, colossal movements of the earth's crust forced the formation upward. This stress produced great breaks in the rock. One of these chunks is the Paunsaugunt Plateau. The fracturing of the rock on the eastern side of the plateau, where Bryce is situated, left it particularly vulnerable to the forces of weather, especially to the slow, steady power of water. These powerful erosive forces are most on display in late winter and early spring. As the ground thaws on warm days, you can hear the grinding, groaning, and grumbling of erosion at work. Water runs down crevices, rocks tumble, and gravel and pebbles shake loose from the sides of the canyon's weird formations.

Bryce Ampitheater

Bryce Amphitheater is the most delectable of the giant shell-shaped bites taken out of the Paunsaugunt Plateau. Several spectacular trails lead down below its rim into a wonderland of rock sculpture. The Peekaboo Loop Trail goes from Bryce Point into the heart of the amphitheater, where the mystery and magic of the Bryce escarpment are at their greatest. As you walk down into the canyon, a formation called the Wall of Windows appears above you. This monstrous slab of limestone has been punctured with gaping holes that let the bright blue sky show through. Below you there is a fantastic array of natural rock carvings that resembles the guests and attendants at a fancy masked ball. The dancers, waiters, musicians, and jesters are presided over by a trio of red-cloaked figures.

Farther on, a broad span of yawning cave mouths, called the Grottos, appears just beneath the rim. The caves have been carved out by water seeping down from the plateau above. Virtually inaccessible to people, the caves offer refuge to red-tailed hawks, ravens, and golden eagles. In the canyon it is easy to get the feeling that this vast piece of the earth was pried open for your personal inspection. You become aware of the emptiness where rock was but no longer is and the spaces once filled with earth and stone that are now open sky.

The Paiute described Bryce Canyon as "red rocks standing like men in a bowl-shaped canyon." Viewed from Bryce Point, the amphitheater certainly appears to be the gathering place for a crowd of giants.

Opposite: *From Bryce Point (8,296 feet high), you can see the Paria River, which shaped Bryce Amphitheater as it gnawed its way into the Paunsaugunt Plateau to collect the streams that are its source.*

In Bryce the endless power of erosion has sculptured thousands of the limestone spires called hoodoos. Derived from the word *voodoo*, the term means "bad luck," but in Bryce Canyon *hoodoo* invokes only the benevolent magic of wondrous shapes and colors. The stunning terra-cotta, yellow, pink, and mauve of the canyon's rock formations result from oxidized chemicals in the stone: Red and yellow come from iron; blue and purple, from manganese. Light also affects the colors of the formations in Bryce. The colors change throughout the day, moving from the blue end of the spectrum in the morning light toward red hues at sunset.

There are 13 overlooks that survey this wonderland. One of the best is Yovimpa Point, a magical rock spur nearly two miles above sea level. From here more than 3,000 square miles of desert fall away to the south. To the east there is a broad sweep of mesas and buttes; to the north, the Aquarius Plateau; and to the south, a descriptively named peak, called Mollie's Nipple.

The view from Rainbow Point (9,105 feet high) reveals the surprisingly dense pine forests that spread out across much of the southern part of the Pausaugunt Plateau.

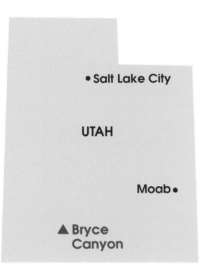

• Salt Lake City

UTAH

Moab •

▲ Bryce Canyon

Bryce In Winter

In winter Bryce Canyon becomes a fairyland. Its thousands of rock hoodoos take on the appearance of magical figures made of red and orange with mantles of white. The park service clears the 15-mile-long scenic drive to Rainbow Point, making this winter wonderland accessible by car. With a permit, snowshoers and cross-country skiers can sleep out-of-doors in designated winter campsites along the Fairyland Loop Trail, the Under-the-Rim Trail (which connects with many of Bryce's shorter paths), and the Riggs Spring Loop Trail. Snowshoes are provided free at the visitor center.

Cross-country skiers cruise along the rim through manzanita, piñon, and ponderosa pines. Skiers who don't mind getting a little snow down their collars venture down the steep trails leading to the canyon floor. There is also winter hiking below the rim for are willing to posthole up to their hips through Utah's deep light powder in exchange for some of the most spectacular winter scenery anywhere on earth.

Bryce Canyon National Park

Established:	1928
Location:	Utah
When to go:	Open all year
Size:	35,835 acres
Terrain:	Forested canyon rim and deep escarpment
Interesting sights:	Wall of Windows and Queen Victoria
Wildlife:	Mule deer, small mammals, reptiles, hawks, golden eagle, and other birds
Activities:	Ranger-led walks and talks, evening programs, night sky programs, moonlight walks, and snowshoe walks; horseback trail rides, hiking, cross-country skiing, snowshoeing, and backpacking (by permit)
Services:	Visitor center, park lodge, and two campgrounds
Information:	Bryce Canyon, Utah 84717; 801-834-5322

Snowfall temporarily softens the rugged terrain viewed from Inspiration Point, 8,143 feet above the canyon floor. When the snow begins to melt, ice and water will carry away another layer of the pink cliffs, revealing ever sharper profiles.

Zion
Monumental Desert Valley

In contrast to the desert around it, the valley of the Virgin River seems to be a lush oasis, but water is as precious here as it is everywhere in the West.

Opposite: *During the late summer, golden buckwheat ripens in a pocket of sandy soil that has collected at the base of a crevice in the Kolob section of the park.*

Right: *Through its striated layers, this masterpiece of natural stone sculpture reveals the long and varied geological history of this region.*

L ong shadows cross the floor of Zion Canyon in the early morning, while sunlight bathes the tops of massive sandstone towers. Mormon settlers gave these natural wonders biblical names, such as the Altar of Sacrifice, the Court of the Patriarchs, and Angels Landing. But even without these appropriately reverential names, the great figures, hulking 2,000 feet above the canyon floor, command our respect and awe. This narrow, curving gorge seems to cut through time itself. Zion is a canyon of spectacular and enormous scale. Its perpendicular cliffs are nearly 3,000 feet high. Its great rock figures are imposing and monolithic, as are the monumental buttresses, deep hanging canyons, rock landings, and alcoves that have been gouged out of the cliff faces. In contrast to this grandeur, the upper end of Zion Canyon, just a few miles away, is so narrow that two people standing side-by-side can both touch the canyon's rock walls. The canyon is so deep that the sun penetrates to its floor for only a brief moment each day.

Unlike other canyon parks, including Canyonlands, Bryce, and the Grand Canyon where many visitors view the canyons from their rims, Zion draws visitors to its floor. From that vantage point, they look up at the stupendous perpendicular topography. Walking along the Virgin River, which created this scenic spectacle, park visitors gain a unique perspective on nature. As they contemplate the great rock figures towering above them from the serenity of groves of Fremont cottonwood, willow, and box elder trees, which line the canyon floor, visitors feel the unusual serenity of this unique place. Here only muted sounds interrupt the special reverence the canyon inspires: the song of a quail, water trickling down a side valley, or the wind blowing through the leaves.

Angels Landing

Angels Landing is a rock pinnacle that rises 1,500 feet above the forested valley floor of Zion Canyon. Visitors reach its airy and stupendous summit by following the West Rim Trail, one of the most beautiful trails in the western United States. It leads through a series of long switchbacks up the canyon wall to Refrigerator Canyon. Many people take a break in a glen of piñon pine and big-tooth maple before negotiating a series of steep switchbacks, called Walters Wiggles.

A sign points to what looks like a nearly impossible route to a narrow ridge that leads to the summit of Angels Landing. The rock drops straight down on either side for more than 1,000 feet, but there are chains strung along the path and footholds cut into the rock to make the trail as safe as possible. The vista from the summit is well worth the effort. It is one of the grandest sights anywhere: a 360-degree view of Zion Canyon. A huge rock monolith, called the Great White Throne, seems to be within a stone's throw on the opposite side, and there is a startling view of what now appears to be a tiny Virgin River meandering through minuscule trees far below.

Zion National Park

Established:	1919
Location:	Utah
When to go:	Open all year (The main season is March through October.)
Size:	146,551 acres
Terrain:	Deep canyon with its rim in high desert plateau
Interesting sight:	Angels Landing
Wildlife:	Mountain lion, mule deer, ring-tailed cat, 270 species of birds, rattlesnake, and reptiles
Activities:	Ranger-led nature walks, talks, evening programs, and children's programs; hiking, horseback trail rides, tram tours, climbing, bicycling, river tubing, cross-country skiing, and backpacking (by permit)
Services:	Two visitor centers, a park lodge, and three campgrounds
Information:	Springdale, Utah 84767; 801-772-3256

This great canyon in the desert has drawn human visitors since ancient times. Archaeological remnants indicate that people lived in the canyon as early as A.D. 500. They were probably wandering groups of weavers who hunted small game and gathered food in the area. Later the Anasazi settled more permanently in the southern end of the canyon, where they built pueblos and irrigation systems to water their crops of corn and beans. The Anasazi disappeared from the area abruptly during the thirteenth century.

In the early-eighteenth century, Spanish priests and soldiers who were exploring the high plateau country north of the Grand Canyon in what is now southwestern Utah came upon the startling canyon. After the arrival of the Spanish explorers, stories of the canyon's wonders began to spread. Later in the century, the famed trapper Jedediah Smith came south from his headquarters to determine the commercial possibilities of the canyon. In the middle of the nineteenth century, several families of Mormon pioneers began using the canyon as a place of special reverence, developing it as a religious retreat.

Zion Canyon was sculptured over the course of a million years by the flowing waters of the Virgin River sifting down through layer after layer of the red and white Navajo sandstone that forms the canyon's sheer walls. The layers of sedimentary sandstone and limestone had been a desert 15 million years ago. Gradually these layers were pushed upwards to form the 1,500-square-mile Markagunt Plateau. Then the Virgin River went to work carving out the monumental canyon. Drawn relentlessly by gravity, it slices its way through the rock down to the desert floor below.

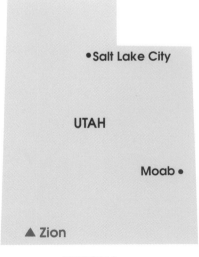

The Great White Throne is a massive sandstone monolith that looms over the canyon floor from a height of 2,450 feet.

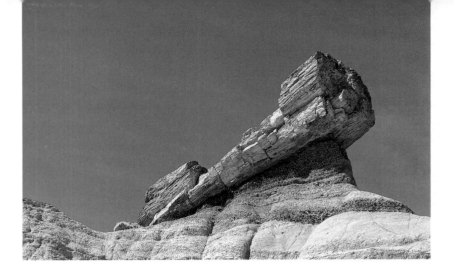

Petrified Forest
Wood of Stone

· ·

The annual rings of this long-extinct relative of the Norfolk Island pine chronicle the weather conditions of the subtropical climate that once existed here.

Opposite: *This area of the park has long been known as the Jasper Forest, but most of the petrified trees found here actually grew some distance away and were washed here by a river.*

Right: *Balanced on the rim of Blue Mesa, this petrified log points to an area in the Painted Desert where trees that lived 200 million years ago were buried.*

In eastern Arizona, a mysterious stretch of bleached badlands is scorched by the blistering sun. This twisted landscape of tortured contours has been eaten away by endless erosion. The forces of nature have carved a high plateau into a jumble of buttes, mesas, gullies, and cones, all tilted at unlikely angles. Vegetation has been reduced to a few bent plants, such as junipers, low-lying shrubs, shortgrasses, and cacti. In spring enormous fields of wildflowers provide a brief respite from the usual barrenness. This landscape seems to have survived from the beginning of time, but perhaps it is a vestige of the end of time. Adding another dimension to the mystery of this other worldly scene, great hulking logs of stone cluster here and there on the ground. Many of the logs are broken into segments so perfectly cut that they look like cordwood felled by a prehistoric giant.

The history of this area goes back more than 200 million years. Aeons ago great herds of dinosaurs roamed through forests of tall conifers, while nearby rivers teemed with armor-scaled fish. The great columns of petrified wood scattered across the desert date from that time. Nature produced the mineralized wood under very special circumstances. The trees were uprooted by great floods or perhaps flows of lava, then washed down from the highlands and buried by silt and volcanic ash. Water seeping through the wood replaced decaying organic material cell by cell with multicolored silica. Eventually, the land where the great logs were buried was lifted up by geological upheaval, and wind and rain began to wear away the overlying sediments, finally exposing the long-buried, now petrified wood.

· ·

The same sediments that petrified the fallen trees also painted the desert with bands of colorful sandstones, shales, and clays.

The Woods Time Forgot

The Petrified Forest is more than large pieces of mineralized trees. It also opens up a window on an environment that is more than 200 million years old. Visitors who walk one of the park's hiking trails get a real sense of this forgotten age. Here it is easy to imagine a marshy wetland where leather-winged pterosaurs soared above rivers filled with giant amphibians and dinosaurs foraged for food on the banks.

Giant Logs Trail leads to the park's largest fossil log, whimsically called Old Faithful. This great multicolored trunk is 170 feet long with a diameter of nearly 10 feet. Long Logs Trail, another walking loop, goes to the park's largest concentration of petrified logs. Some of the logs are more than 150 feet long; all are piled in a great logjam. Other trails lead deeper into the park, giving visitors an even firmer grasp of the past.

Each piece of wood is unique, burning with the colors of the Painted Desert of which Petrified Forest National Park is a part. Some of the great trunks still bear the annual rings that reveal their life histories in prehistoric times. The Paiute believed that the petrified logs were the great arrow shafts of their thunder god, Shinauv. The Navajo said they were the bones of a mythological giant, called Yietso. After American explorers found these great "stone trees" in the mid-nineteenth century, a steady stream of visitors began making the trek to Petrified Forest. A military survey party passed through the region in 1851, and its members filled their saddlebags with pieces of the petrified wood. By about 1870 great quantities of glistening rock were being carried off by souvenir hunters and commercial developers, who cut slabs from the logs for tabletops and mantles. Petrified wood was also blasted apart in search of valuable amethysts or quartz crystals that some of the wood contains. A mill was built to grind the great logs into abrasives. Concerned citizens went to the Arizona Territorial Legislature to seek federal protection for the area, and Petrified Forest was declared a national monument in 1906.

The southern section of the park contains one of the world's largest concentrations of petrified wood. Here great logs of jasper and agate are interspersed with smaller pieces and fragments glistening in the sun like immense jewels. The northern part of the park encompasses the colorful mesas and buttes of the Painted Desert. Here sun, sand, and rock create a dazzling range of color and pattern.

Petrified Forest National Park

Established:	1962
Location:	Arizona
When to go:	Open all year
Size:	93,533 acres
Terrain:	Desert and badlands
Interesting sights:	Old Faithful and the Painted Desert
Wildlife:	Kangaroo and pack rat, turkey vulture, coyote, canyon mouse, and rattlesnake
Activities:	Ranger-led nature walks, interpretive exhibits, self-guided auto tours, horseback riding, hiking, and backpacking
Services:	Two visitor centers, a museum, and food service
Information:	P.O. Box 217, Petrified Forest, Arizona 86028; 602-524-6228

The eroded sides of beautiful Blue Mesa clearly reveal the layers of sediment in the ancient marsh that buried and transformed the petrified logs.

Grand Canyon
Time and the River

· ·

Today the once-red Colorado River runs green because the Glen Canyon Dam disrupts its flow, allowing about 80 percent of the silt that the river used to carry to settle in Lake Powell.

Opposite: *The Paiute believed that the god Tavwoats opened the canyon as a path to the land beyond death. For modern geologists the Grand Canyon is a path that leads back to the beginnings of our planet.*

Right: *The silver orb of the setting moon highlights the unworldly immensity of Grand Canyon, as the first blush of dawn spreads out along the canyon's rim.*

The true magnificence of Grand Canyon takes all visitors by surprise. You approach the canyon from the south across a gently rising plateau or from the north across higher and wilder country. Nothing in the topography on either side gives you a hint of what is soon to unfold. Suddenly you are there, standing on the rim of one of the most sublime and profound spectacles on this planet. The chasm is so vast and so deep that on first sight it looks as though the earth has opened to allow us to glimpse the secrets that lie at its greatest depths.

The scale of the canyon is immense, and even from the best vantage points, only a small fraction of its 277 miles can be seen. Nobody has seen all of the Grand Canyon, despite the fact that millions and millions of people from around the globe have been here. Most visitors first view this truly unbelievable sight from the more accessible South Rim, which offers a stunning view into the deep inner gorge of the Colorado River. From here the vista is so dramatic that it can be overwhelming. What you see extending for a mile down below your feet are millions of years of geologic history. Nowhere else on earth can you view such a complete history of the geologic workings of the planet laid out so clearly and so orderly.

Some of the earth's oldest rock lies at the bottom of Grand Canyon. This rock may have formed about the same time that the first spark of life was ignited on earth. Thousands of feet thick, the rock is made up of sediments. About 300 million years after it formed, monumental geologic forces lifted the rock up into a great range of mountains that may have been six miles high, or about the height of the Himalayas. Over time the mountains eroded into a plain. About one billion years ago, that

· ·

plain was raised into a second mountain range. These mountains also were worn away by millions of years of rain, wind, and frost. During later ages the entire region sank beneath an inland sea, with primitive shellfish fossilizing in sea bottoms that eventually hardened to shale. Aeons later the region rose again as a high plateau; the former sea bottom was now on top and the ancient rocks below. This is when the Colorado River went to work, first cutting into the upper layers about six million years ago. Carving inch by inch over the millennia, the river finally reached the oldest rocks nearly a mile below the surface.

People lived in the canyon centuries ago, but the first white men to explore the area were 13 members of Coronado's expedition. They arrived in about 1540. One wrote a letter of official disgust at the fact that his expedition had encountered an unbridgeable barrier to further exploration. In the 1850s the army sent a surveying party

Running the Colorado

Once you have seen the Grand Canyon from the rim and taken in its vastness and mystery, you may get the kind of feeling about the place that has turned many onlookers into explorers. After you have had enough of the big view, you may want to see the inner canyon for yourself. One of the most exciting ways to experience the canyon is by raft or dory trip down the Colorado. These trips vary in length from about three days by motorized raft to 18 days or more by unpowered dories, which are similar to those used by John Wesley Powell, whose journals are still used as guides by modern river runners.

Offered by a number of river companies, the trips cover long, quiet stretches of deep water through the heart of the canyon, with stops for overnight camping at several scenic or unusual sights along the way and day hikes to ruins, waterfalls, side canyons, and tributary streams. The river journey is broken by more than 140 major rapids. At least two of these are hand-clenching, jaw-tightening swirls of cascading water and thunderous waves that are rated 10 on a scale of 10. Is the trip worth the challenge? Almost everybody who travels downriver through the great canyon regards it as the experience of a lifetime.

Curtains of smooth sandstone appear to have been drawn open to reveal this small waterfall that runs out of North Canyon.

Opposite: *The Colorado River flows calmly through the canyon 3,000 feet below Toroweap Point on the North Rim. In this area Grand Canyon is only a half mile wide.*

into the area, but in 1869 John Wesley Powell, a one-armed army major, became the first modern player in the canyon's history. Powell set out with a small party in four boats to explore as much of the length of the Colorado River and the canyon as he could. It was a fearful journey that cost the major two of his boats. But he proved that the canyon could be explored. Accounts of his bold river run were widely published, leading to increased public interest in the Southwest. By the 1880s a prospector named John Hance, known for a quick wit and tall tales, had begun leading sightseeing parties into the canyon.

Today the national park, which was established in 1919, following years of intense campaigning, draws visitors to two major areas, the South Rim and the North Rim, which is wilder and about 1,000 feet higher. Theodore Roosevelt called the Grand Canyon the "one great sight" every American should see. Today, according to several surveys, most Americans and many foreign visitors want to see the Grand Canyon more than any other sight in the United States.

Looking down from Yavapai Point, you can see that the river runs closer to the South Rim. This is because the land tilts to the south and because the more abundant water on the North Rim erodes the canyon faster.

Left: *Early visitors to Grand Canyon assigned the names of the ancient gods and goddesses to many of its monumental formations. Seen at sunrise from Cape Royal, this formation on the North Rim was named for Freya, the Norse goddess of love and beauty.*

155

Into the Canyon

If you want a different perspective on the Grand Canyon than you can get standing on the rim, you must take one of several spectacular trails that lead down into the canyon from both the North Rim and the South Rim. The popular Bright Angel Trail goes in eight miles from the South Rim down to the Phantom Ranch, a lodge and campground clustered among a glen of Fremont cottonwoods on the canyon floor.

Another alternative is the famous or infamous, depending upon your viewpoint, muleback ride through the natural wonders of the canyon. The mules depart from the South Rim for both day trips and overnight pack trips to Phantom Ranch, where guests stay in rustic cabins and dormitories. This is the only place within the canyon itself where you can spend a night and not camp out. The ranch lies in a deep gorge of the inner canyon near the place where Bright Angel Creek joins the Colorado River.

As you journey down into the canyon on the back of your small but sturdy mule, you will have plenty of time to observe a variety of plant and animal life that you could otherwise only see by traveling from the Sonoran Desert of Mexico to the shore of Canada's Hudson Bay. The canyon's great depth contains such a range of temperature and precipitation that the variety of local climates equals the natural scope of nearly the entire continent. These life zones mostly occur in the order you would expect, but in some places the desert zone is higher than the Canadian zone because the canyon's topography can make a high area hot and a low one cool.

The steep switchbacks of Bright Angel Trail, which lead visitors into the canyon from the South Rim, used to convey Native Americans to a cottonwood oasis 3,100 feet below.

• •

Grand Canyon National Park

Established:	1919
Location:	Arizona
When to go:	Open all year. (North Rim is closed late-October to mid-May.)
Size:	1,218,375 acres
Terrain:	High desert plateau and vast canyonland
Interesting sights:	Phantom Ranch and North Rim
Wildlife:	Bighorn sheep, deer, cottontail rabbit, Kaibab and ground squirrel, rattlesnake, spiny lizard, small mammals, reptiles, and birds
Activities:	Ranger-led nature walks, talks, slide shows, and campfire programs; horse and mule trips, hiking, bicycling, fishing, river rafting, air tours, cross-country skiing, and backpacking
Services:	Two visitor centers, seven lodges, and four campgrounds
Information:	P.O. Box 129, Grand Canyon, Arizona 86023; 602-638-7888

Winter quiets the Grand Canyon, spreading a thin blanket of snow over its heights and slowing the steady stream of visitors who come through the park during the rest of the year.

Great Basin
Endless Horizon

I n a corner of the vast territory that stretches across the West between the Rocky Mountains and the Sierra Nevada, an unexpectedly rugged landscape suddenly rises above the floor of the desert into the great blue sky of eastern Nevada. Peaks and hills carved by glaciers from a Pleistocene ice age tower more than a mile above the flat surface. Across the forest-covered flanks of the mountains are piles of rocks left by ancient glaciers. Great Basin also holds alpine lakes, rollicking streams and rivers, and lovely green meadows filled with many varieties of wildflowers.

Great Basin was named by John C. Fremont who led the first party of white explorers into this territory in the mid-nineteenth century. Although maps make it look like a basin because two great boundary mountain ranges give it definition to the east and west, the region actually consists of more than 100 valleys. The newest national park that lies within the boundaries of the 50 states, Great Basin, takes in only a small part of this vast expanse of land, which includes some of the nation's most geologically fascinating terrain.

Great Basin National Park offers visitors solitude and sweeping views of the basin and range country that lies within and outside its boundaries. The centerpiece of the park is Wheeler Peak, Nevada's second tallest mountain at 13,063 feet. The main park road travels up to the 10,000-foot level on the mountain. From there a trail leads to a stand of bristlecone pines, the world's oldest living trees. They look ancient indeed with their twisted, gnarled trunks and their bark carved and polished like rock by aeons of wind, snow, and ice. The trees are vestiges of a Pleistocene forest that once covered the region. Bristlecones

At the limit of the timberline, 4,000-year-old bristlecone pines, survive in an incredibly hostile climate of harsh winters and lengthy annual droughts.

Opposite: *Idyllic Baker Lake is fed by Baker Creek that flows out of a glaciated canyon on Wheeler Peak.*

Right: *Rising several thousand feet above the timberline, Wheeler Peak, which at 13,063 feet is one of the highest mountains in Nevada, often wears a mantle of snow on its barren summit.*

are survivors and continue to live even after most of their trunks and branches die, sustained by minuscule amounts of moisture. Some of the trees in the park are more than 3,000 years old; they were alive when the pharaohs ruled Egypt. One tree named Prometheus lived for nearly 5,000 years before it was cut down in 1964.

Lehman Caves is on the lower slopes of Wheeler Peak at an altitude of about 6,800 feet. The caverns are an underground wonderland filled with intricate and spectacular formations. There are about one and a half miles of trails in the caves through which rangers lead visitors. The caverns are filled with latticed columns, undulating draperies, helicotites, and stalactites. These formations are so dense that the caves' first explorers took along sledgehammers to clear a trail. Among its many treasures, Lehman Caves contains excellent examples of cave shields. These large and rare disks grow out of ceiling cracks where seeping mineral-laden water deposits sediments in flat circular shapes. There is even a small community of pack rats, cave crickets, and strange endemic spiders with scorpionlike pincers living in the caves.

Great Basin National Park

Established:	1986
Location:	Nevada
When to go:	Open all year. (Winter access is limited.)
Size:	77,109 acres
Terrain:	High desert and alpine
Interesting sights:	Wheeler Peak and Lehman Caves
Wildlife:	Bighorn sheep, mule deer, coyote, small mammals, dozens of bird species, and rattlesnake
Activities:	Ranger-led nature walks and talks, campfire programs, cave tours, candlelight cave tours, and spelunking trips; Wheeler Peak scenic drive, hiking, fishing, climbing, cross-country skiing, and backpacking
Services:	Visitor center and four campgrounds
Information:	Baker, Nevada 89311; 702-234-7331

NEVADA

• Reno

Great Basin ▲

• Salt Lake City

UTAH

Las Vegas •

Up Wheeler Peak

The only glacier in Great Basin lies near the 13,063-foot summit of lovely Wheeler Peak, close to a stand of bristlecone pine trees. The summit can be reached by car and on foot. From the main park road, visitors follow a trail that leads up the mountain to the Wheeler Peak Campground. Along the way the environment changes from a piñon and juniper forest, which is able to withstand drought, to a high-altitude world of spruce, pine, and aspen. At the 10,000-foot level, visitors have a choice of several trails into the park's backcountry or a trail to the peak's summit 3,000 feet above.

One of the most popular hikes is the three-mile Alpine Lakes Loop Trail that leads to a spectacularly scenic alpine setting, with a ragged mountain ridge rising high above a lake. Another trail follows the ridge up to the summit, which is populated by pikas and marmots and decorated with wildflowers poking out of niches in the rock.

From Wheeler Peak a rugged desert stretches endlessly to the west, but the higher elevation and increased moisture bless the foothills of Wheeler with stands of tall trees.

Parachute formations are unique to Lehman Cave, but no one has yet been able to explain exactly how dripping water containing calcium carbonate creates these unusual shapes.

Redwood
Land of Tall Trees

There is no biological reason why redwood trees should ever die; their bark resists insects, fungus, and fire. But the once-vast redwood forests have been almost destroyed because the trees make exceptionally fine lumber.

Opposite: *The foggy California coast nurtures Del Norte redwoods with the warm moist air they require. The trees prosper in a five to 20 mile wide band between the Pacific Ocean and the coast range.*

Right: *During June and July, California roseberry, a kind of rhododendron, brightens the forest with brilliant flashes of intense pink.*

T his is a forest of startlingly immense proportion. Full-grown adults look like miniature toy figures next to these great trees that soar 30 stories into the sky, higher than any other living things on earth. To put their height in perspective, the redwoods are taller than the torch of the Statue of Liberty. The first branches of these trees begin 100 to 200 feet above the spongy, forest floor. They form a delicate green canopy that seems to push the blue sky even higher than it usually seems in the West. California's mighty redwood trees, many now living in their second millennia, are the last large stands of these monumental conifers that flourished all across North America during the lush, humid period before the last ice age. Here, near the Pacific Ocean, the gentle climate still sustains them.

Today the mighty trees grow in dense groves in a fog belt along the coast, especially in the canyons and river valleys that open directly to the ocean. Scientists have only recently begun to understand the complex ecosystem of these ancient redwood forests. The branches that form the canopy at the top of the redwoods eventually fall to earth where they mix with leaves and branches from hemlock and other species and decay. This process sustains a rich web of life. The trees on which some animals depend in turn depend upon other species of animals. For example, a species of vole eat the fruiting bodies of fungi on dead logs, then excrete the spores on new sites. The spores grow new fungi that are necessary to carry nutrients and moisture to seedlings and tree roots. Owls, flying squirrels, pileated woodpeckers, and martens nest in dead trees and find food throughout the forest.

In the late-nineteenth and early-twentieth centuries, loggers pushed westward across the continent, cutting down mile after mile of the nation's primeval forests. Today almost all of the old-growth forests are gone. The ancient tress that remain are found along the Pacific, where only about one-fifth of the original 15 million acres of trees that once blanketed the region still stand. Unfortunately for these stately giants of the forest, the demand for lumber from redwoods has always been great because the wood resists shrinkage, rot, and decay.

At the beginning of the century, a league to save the redwood was formed. Aided by the state, the league was able to acquire hundreds of stands and include them in 26 state parks where they would be preserved. When Redwood National Park was created in 1968, it incorporated three of these parks, Jedediah Smith, Del Norte Coast, and Prairie Creek, with a total of about 58,000 acres. In 1978 Congress added an additional 48,000 acres to the original acreage, including 36,000 acres that already had been logged. One park official described this area as looking like an "active war zone." Today the clear-cut area is being reclaimed for redwood trees. Officials estimate that it will take 50 years for the logging scars to disappear and another 250 years for the new redwoods to grow to modest size.

When a redwood falls in the forest, usually as a result of erosion around its roots, its decaying wood nourishes saplings and the rent in the forest canopy allows maples and other small trees to grow.

Redwood National Park

Established:	1968
Location:	California
When to go:	Open all year
Size:	110,132 acres
Terrain:	Rolling redwood forests and coastal plain
Interesting sight:	Tall Tree
Wildlife:	Elk, deer, rabbit, owl, marten, and woodpecker
Activities:	Ranger-led tide-pool and seashore walks, and evening programs; hiking, canoeing, guided kayak trips, horseback riding, fishing, swimming, whale watching, and backpacking
Services:	Visitor center, information center, and four campgrounds
Information:	1111 Second Street, Crescent City, California 95531; 707-464-6101

Redwood

Eureka

Sacramento

San Francisco

CALIFORNIA

Los Angeles

Tall Trees Grove

Tall Trees Grove, the centerpiece of Redwood National Park, is part of a stupendous stretch of unusually tall redwoods that is called the Emerald Mile. Here, under a vaulted green canopy, sunshine reaches the forest floor only in splintered shafts of light, creating an effect that resembles a gothic cathedral, where great columns of stone are punctuated by stained glass. The mystery of this magical place is further heightened when fog rolls in from the nearby ocean, wrapping the great trees in a wispy gauze of vapor.

Among the giants in Tall Trees Grove stands the world's tallest known tree, appropriately called the Tall Tree. Its top rises almost 368 feet above the ground; its circumference is 44 feet. Foresters estimate that the tree is about 600 years old. This remarkable tree was not measured until 1963 when it was discovered, along with the second and third tallest trees, which stand nearby.

Grassy bluffs, a rock-strewn beach, and the well-known coastal landmark of Split Rock identify the western boundary of Redwood National Park.

Lassen Volcanic
Land of Scorched Earth

• •

In this vast panorama of devastated landscape, volcanism displays its spectacular and destructive artistry. Lassen Volcanic National Park is evidence of the incredible violence that lies below the surface of our planet. The last eruptions occurred here early in this century, but Lassen still has an otherworldly terrain of broken mountains, scorched land, bubbling mud pots, and hissing steam.

Lassen is at the southern end of the Cascade Mountains, which contains other volcanic peaks, Mount Rainier, Mount Shasta, and Mount St. Helens. This national park is a churned-up landscape of stark features that have been given such descriptive names as Chaos Crags and Chaos Jumbles. At one spot, intriguingly called Bumpass Hell, powerful-smelling vapors drift over boiling hot springs with golden flakes floating on their surface. The flakes are crystals of iron pyrite, or fool's gold, that have been carried along by superheated steam.

Visitors to the park amble through dense sulphur fumes to see thick gurgling clay, tinted pastel colors with minerals from far below the earth's surface. The centerpiece of the park is Lassen Peak, a volcano that erupted 150 times over a one-year period beginning in 1914. The peak was once part of a much larger volcano, called Mt. Tehama. Today Lassen is a 10,457-foot-high pile of gray volcanic rock, which is covered by snow much of the year. It is so barren of life that it has been called a "vertical dessert," but watchful hikers on the trail to its summit sometimes see a ground squirrel or a swarm of tortoiseshell butterflies.

• •

In a fumarole at Bumpass Hell, thick gooey mud boils much like oatmeal in a pot. When an air bubble rises to the surface, it bursts with a plop, splattering hot mud in all directions.

Opposite: *Reflected in the clear water of Manzanita Lake and sprinkled with fresh snow, Lassen Peak's serene looks belie the volcano's recent history of violent and devastating eruptions.*

Right: *Bumpass Hell is a mile-wide valley where thermal activity fills the air with sulfurous steam and pools can be as hot as 196 degrees Fahrenheit.*

167

Today the park is a natural laboratory that spectacularly displays the effects of past volcanic action as well as the on-going turmoil beneath the earth's surface. Throughout the park, cinder crags and magma canyons offer proof of former violence, while gurgling fumaroles and sulphur fumes suggest the possibility of a fiery future. In one place, appropriately called the Devastated Area, scorched and fallen trees dot the landscape amid such signs of renewal as saplings, grass, and stubborn new bushes.

The Cinder Cone, a nearly cylindrical mountain of lava, rises ominously above the pine forest. The cone formed as it emitted lava and ash that then fell back onto its slopes as multicolored cinders. The crater at the top of the Cinder Cone dates to its most recent eruption in 1851. That display of natural fireworks was seen more than 100 miles away. Manzanita Lake also adds to the drama of the park's furious landscape. Geologists believe that the lake was formed about three centuries ago when a volcanic dome suddenly collapsed, possibly as the result of an earthquake. Riding a gigantic cushion of trapped air, millions of tons of rock and debris flew across about two miles of flat terrain. Finally the horizontal landslide was stopped by a mountain, where it blocked a creek to form the lake.

• •

Lassen Volcanic National Park

Established:	1916
Location:	California
When to go:	Open all year. (Winter access is limited.)
Size:	106,372 acres
Wildlife:	Deer, ground squirrel, small mammals, and birds
Terrain:	Scoured volcanic landscape, lakes, and mountains
Interesting sights:	Lassen Peak and Cinder Cone
Activities:	Ranger-led nature walks and talks, children's and evening programs; hiking, swimming, fishing, boating, field seminars, cross-country and downhill skiing, and backpacking
Services:	Visitor center, guest ranch, and eight campgrounds
Information:	P.O. Box 100, Mineral, California 96063; 916-595-4444

Lassen Peak

Lassen Peak was once part of a much larger mountain that began 200,000 or more years ago as molten rock, called magma, flowed upwards from the depths of the earth. Slowly over the years and layer by layer, the magma formed an immense cone 15 miles wide and 11,500 feet high. Over thousands of years, the great volcano collapsed, giving birth to smaller mountains around its rim. Lassen Peak is one of these mountains. It is a plug volcano made of stiff lumps of lava pushed upward by powerful geologic forces.

In the mid-nineteenth century, when the first settlers came to California, the area around the peak was dotted with bubbling springs and vents spewing steam. But the peak itself appeared calm. The newcomers assumed the volcano was extinct. In May 1914 the peak showed signs of life, pouring forth enormous columns of steam and gases from its top. Three scientists decided to climb to the summit to see if they could determine whether the volcano would erupt. As they peered down into a new crater near the top, they felt the ground rumbling beneath them. They turned and fled down the mountain, barely surviving the blast. Lassen erupted 150 more times during the next year. Finally in May 1915, the mountaintop exploded. Lava poured down the slopes, and a blast of ash and gas shot out of the volcano, rising 30,000 feet in the air and devastating a three-square-mile area.

Since then, except for a small eruption in 1921, the volcano has remained dormant. Until Mount St. Helens exploded in 1980, Lassen was the last eruption in the lower 48 states. Scientists are now studying the devastated landscape around Lassen to see how long it is likely to take for the burned and barren slopes of Mount St. Helens to recover. Today a trail leads to the summit of Lassen Peak. From here there are fine views of the bleak and darkened remains of the 1915 eruption as well as the cone of another volcano, Mt. Shasta, 75 miles to the northwest.

Lassen Peak is currently 10,457 feet high and almost totally placid, but Lassen is not the first volcano to rise in this area, and like its predecessors, it may someday blow itself apart.

Yosemite
Sculpted by Ice

· ·

The spectacularly beautiful natural setting of Yosemite Valley inspired one of its first explorers to write, "As I looked at the grandeur of the scene, a peculiar exalted sensation seemed to fill my whole being, and I found my eyes in tears with emotion." Visitors today find themselves equally moved by this profoundly lovely gorge, cut by the Merced River, with its sides gouged out by glaciers into enormous monoliths. Here granite cliffs rise 3,000 feet above a forested floor, a tranquil and solemn river flows grandly through its proud channel, and waterfalls tumble from the heights. The famed Yosemite Fall is 2,425 feet high, which makes it North America's highest waterfall.

The grandeur of Yosemite tugs at the soul. A park ranger was once asked what he would do if he had only one day to visit Yosemite Valley. The ranger replied, "I'd weep." Whether apocryphal or not, the anecdote contains much truth about this grassy, tree-filled defile cut deep into the heart of the Sierra Nevada. Although it contains less than one half of one percent of the total area of the park, this valley is undoubtedly what most people think of when they think of Yosemite. The gorge is guarded by two famous sentinel rocks; their massive shapes are well known around the globe. The park's most famous landmark, Half Dome, with its great sheared-off face, rises 4,800 feet above the eastern end of the valley. El Capitan, a monolith that rises 3,600 feet above the evergreens along the Merced River, stands sentinel at the western entrance. One of the most precipitous cliffs in the world, El Capitan, which in Spanish means "the chief," is made of granite so hard and crack free that the powerful forces of erosion scarcely seem to affect it.

· ·

To some people, including the Ahwahneechee who lived in this naturally fortified valley for centuries, El Capitan looks like the head of a rock chief, or captain.

Opposite: *The symmetrical gothic towers of Cathedral Rocks, across the valley from El Capitan, are so massive that they almost eclipse diaphanous Bridalveil Fall, which is 620 feet high and the only waterfall in the park that never dries up in the summer.*

Right: *The Merced River cuts a mighty course through the Yosemite Valley, with a force that contradicts its name that comes from Nuestra Señora de la Merced, Our Lady of Mercy.*

Pioneer Yosemite History Center

Along with its spectacular geology, Yosemite has a fascinating history to tell. At Wawona, near the south entrance, the Pioneer Yosemite History Center gives visitors a real sense of the past. Restored buildings have the look and feel of the nineteenth century. Visitors can chat with costumed guides who portray homesteaders, cavalry officers, farmers, and mountaineers.

One of the stories you are likely to hear at the history center relates the origin of the name Yosemite. According to the tale, when the Mariposa Battclion tracked an Ahwahneechee war party accused of raiding nearby mountain trading posts into the valley, the warriors yelled something that sounded like "Yo Shay Ma Tee" or "Yo Ha Mi Tee." This meant "some of them are killers" and was an expression usually reserved for grizzly bears not other people. Apparently thinking this was the Ahwahneechee name for the area, the soldiers gave an approximation of it to the glorious valley.

Yosemite Fall leaps down a sheer rock face in a series of cascades that looks like a single mighty waterfall. At 2,425 feet tall, it is the highest waterfall in North America.

Beyond this justifiably famous valley, the park is a showcase for the wonders of nature. This vast and varied domain includes giant sequoias, alpine meadows, Sierra peaks soaring above 13,000 feet, lovely alpine lakes, sparkling trout streams, grassy meadows, and glacial remnants. The range of natural features is so diverse because of Yosemite's location in the temperate climate of central California and an unusually varied terrain, ranging from desert to high alpine. Within the park, there are four of the seven life zones found on the North American continent. At its lowest elevations, a desertlike environment harbors the brush rabbit and chaparral. Next are mid-elevation forests and the valley floors that provide a haven for mule deer and chipmunks. Moving up in altitude, the red fir and Jeffrey pine of high-elevation forests take over. This is where deer and the park's resident black bears migrate in spring. Higher still is a colder and harsher subalpine world. This land is dominated by rock, snow, and ice. Where soil has been able to cover the rocky landscape, meadows grow, providing a habitat for such small animals as the marmot and pika. Dwarf willows and dozens of wildflower species dot the alpine meadows. Tuolumne Meadows, one of the park's most famed and cherished features, is a vast expanse of flowing grass, cut by the lovely Tuolumne River and circled by peaks of the Sierra. Millions of years ago, the meadow was under a vast sheet of ice nearly half a mile thick. Today a riot of wildflowers sprouts in spring.

The park contains three groves of giant sequoias. These great towering monuments of another age are second only to bristlecone pine trees in age among all living things. Each of the groves, which are widely separated by less lofty forests of pine and ponderosa, contains several hundred giant trees. The best known of the three, Mariposa Grove, has about 200 sequoia trees, which rise so far above the thick, bouncy forest floor that you are only dimly aware of their tops. One of the trees is called the Grizzly Giant. It is believed to be the oldest sequoia, and it is the fifth largest tree in the world. Grizzly Giant is estimated to be 2,700 years old; its weight is 1,000 tons, and its top rises more than 200 feet above the ground.

Separated by about 35 miles from each other, Mariposa Grove and Yosemite Valley played seminal roles in the

Yosemite's gigantic sequoias grow in mixed evergreen forests among white firs that resemble tall Christmas trees, Jeffrey pines, and other trees.

history of America's national parks. Native Americans had known about the wonders of Yosemite Valley for centuries, but it was not discovered by white men until the mid-nineteenth century. This startling piece of wilderness wonderland was probably first viewed from the rim as early as the 1830s, but the first white men to enter the valley were a pair of '49er miners who were tracking a wounded bear. In 1851 an army battalion entered the valley in pursuit of Ahwahneechee warriors, and by 1855 the first tourist wagons were creaking through the valley over old Indian trails. Soon afterwards toll roads and hotels were opened by local entrepreneurs.

In 1864 President Abraham Lincoln signed a bill giving Mariposa Grove and Yosemite Valley to the state of California to protect in perpetuity. This was the first time any nation had established a wilderness preserve within its own boundaries. Following the creation of Yellowstone National Park in 1872, early conservationists, particularly John Muir, urged that Yosemite also be established as a national park. The park was finally mandated in 1890, but it was administered as two separate state parks for 16 more years. Thanks to the foresight of President Lincoln, John Muir, and others, the park remains sublimely beautiful, an incomparable masterpiece of nature.

After a rough and tumble course down the Grand Stairway, over Nevada and Vernal falls, and through a half-mile stretch where it drops 1,200 feet, the Merced River levels out on the valley floor with a lazy majesty.

Opposite: *Contrary to appearances, there never was another half of Half Dome, and the quartz monzonite outcropping was not rounded by glaciers. The shape of Half Dome is the result of exfoliation, a process by which rock sheds its outer layers along fault lines.*

174

Construction of El Capitan

Yosemite Valley was formed by glaciers during a Pleistocene ice age. At the beginning of the epoch, the terrain now occupied by the Sierra Nevada was covered with low ridges, hills, and valleys. An ancient predecessor of the Merced River flowed through this quiet landscape. Over aeons a gradual upheaval powered by awesome geologic forces beneath the earth tilted the Sierra block. This caused the fledgling river to pick up speed and rush toward the sea. As its flow increased in velocity, the river began carving its way down through the bedrock. Eventually a 2,000-foot V-shaped valley was cut. Millions of years later, the climate changed, and great ice sheets began spreading across the area and into the valley. Over time the glaciers ground the valley into a steep U-shaped defile, rounding peaks along its sides into great domes. Advancing and receding three times, the glaciers eventually melted, leaving a lake-covered valley. In time the lake disappeared.

The result of all this erosion is a flat-bottomed, forested valley floor with monumental monoliths rising above sheared canyon walls. The famous domed rock, El Capitan, is larger than the Rock of Gibraltar. Geologists believe it may be the largest single block of granite in the world. Today its spectacular 3,000-foot face draws rock climbers from around the world. From the valley floor, visitors often see the tiny figures of climbers making the daring assent of the cliff. During the climb that takes several days, they sleep in slings hanging from minuscule cracks or ledges in the cliff face.

Yosemite National Park

Established:	1890
Location:	California
When to go:	Open all year. (Winter access is limited.)
Size:	761,170 acres
Terrain:	Deep gorge, forests, mountains, and meadows
Interesting sights:	El Capitan, Mariposa Grove, and Yosemite Fall
Wildlife:	Mule deer, bear, squirrel, rabbit, marmot, pika, and dozens of bird species
Activities:	Ranger-led talks and walks, evening and children's programs, bike rides, and history tours; auto tape tours, bus and tram tours, stagecoach rides, films, plays, concerts, art and photography classes, music workshops, museum, horseback riding, climbing, fishing, rafting, swimming, boating, ice-skating, cross-country and downhill skiing, and backpacking
Services:	Two visitor centers, history center, nature center, seven lodges, cabins, and 15 campgrounds
Information:	P.O. Box 577, Yosemite, California 95389; 209-372-0200

Of this magnificent valley, John Muir wrote: "These sacred mountain temples are the holiest ground that the heart of man has consecrated."

Shimmering Mirror Lake in Tenaya Canyon will eventually become a grassy meadow and then a forest, because debris brought in by the river is gradually filling the lake, causing it to dry up.

Sequoia-Kings Canyon
High Mountains, Big Trees

If national parks had themes, the theme of this park would be bigness: big trees, big mountains, and big canyons. The park contains the planet's largest living things, giant sequoia trees that are so huge they far outstrip the size of any other species. Lofty Mount Whitney at 14,495 feet is the highest mountain in the lower 48 states. Kings Canyon plunges down steep granite walls more than 8,000 feet from its rim to the Kings River below, making it the deepest canyon in North America. It is more than half again as deep as the Grand Canyon.

Sequoia is America's second national park. It was established in 1890 as a wilderness sanctuary to protect groves of giant sequoia trees that were being destroyed by logging. Kings Canyon, a steep-walled valley, was mandated as a national park in 1940, absorbing General Grant National Park that had been created by Congress almost as an afterthought just three weeks after it approved neighboring Sequoia. Today these two adjacent parks are unique within the National Park System. Since 1943 they have been administered jointly, a single, huge park with two names that encompasses most of California's High Sierra country. This startling parkland contains thousands of acres of sequoias and some of the nation's wildest and loveliest alpine scenery. Here are miles of sweeping mountain vistas, range after range of snow-capped peaks, high meadows, rocky ridges, and green forests of pine and ponderosa.

The largest trees by weight and volume in the world, the sequoias in this park are the last relic of a species that covered

Scooped out of Kings Canyon by a glacier during the most recent ice age, peaceful Zumwalt Meadow spreads out below the towering heights of North Dome (8,717 feet high).

Opposite: *Looking at these immense trees, it is hard to believe that the seeds of the sequoia are so tiny that 91,000 of them weigh only one pound.*

Right: *The half-mile walk up Moro Rock (6,725 feet high) rewards park visitors with this spectacular view of Castle Rocks (9,180 feet high) and extensive sequoia forests.*

much of the world before the most recent ice age. The glaciers swept over all but a few thousand acres too high in the Sierra Nevada for the ice to reach, destroying all the trees in their path. Sequoias used to be considered a subspecies of the coast redwoods that are found in Redwood National Park and elsewhere. The scientific term for the redwood tree is *Sequoia sempervirens*—a name that came from Sequoyah, the inventor of the Cherokee alphabet, who was much admired by the Austrian botanist who named the redwoods. The same name was at first also given to the giant trees of the Sierra Nevada. Today botanists realize the Sierra Nevada sequoia is a separate species. They now call it *Sequoia gigantea*.

The groves of these huge trees seem to go on forever, but these sequoia forests are almost nothing compared with what existed here just a little over a century ago. Logging of what was then one of the world's finest and most extensive old-growth forests began in about 1862 and continued relentlessly until the turn of the century. Vast stands of these giant trees were wiped out, including at least two trees, and possibly as many as four, that were bigger than the biggest tree in the world today, the park's famed General Sherman sequoia. Two of these trees were cut for a reason that today seems frivolous. Their trunks were put on display at world's fairs. In the park you can still see the Centennial Stump, the remains of a gigantic sequoia cut down for exhibition at the 1875 Centennial in Philadelphia. Nearby is the Big Stump Trail, a one-mile path that leads through a wasteland of downed logs, stumps, and fallen trees, which are reminders of an earlier era when these giants were only valued for their wood.

The bigness of the park that is evident in these great trees is also reflected in its spectacular alpine backcountry. This park is almost completely wilderness. Its boundaries encompass most of the Sierra Nevada. These mountains are the longest and highest unbroken range in North America, stretching more than 400 miles from north to south. A jagged, sawtooth chain of rocky ridges punctuated by sheared granite peaks, the section of the Sierra Nevada within Sequoia and Kings Canyon is not a range of individual mountains but a great upheaval of solid granite. Its western side rises somewhat gradually from foothills to more than 13,000 feet, then plummets

The General Sherman sequoia, the world's largest tree, is mostly trunk. Its lower limbs all died because the immense tree prevented them from getting enough sunlight.

The General Sherman Tree

The statistics of the General Sherman sequoia, the biggest living thing on earth, are staggering. Its bulk, estimated at four and a half million pounds, far exceeds any other tree on earth. Its 275-foot height, although it is not as tall as some redwood trees, is certainly respectable. Its lowest branch is 130 feet above the ground, which is high enough that a 12-story building would not reach it. This branch, incidentally, is itself larger than any tree in the United States east of the Mississippi River.

The General may be as old as 2,500 years, and it is still growing. Botanists believe that the tree adds enough wood each year to build another 60-foot-tall tree. The total lumber contained within the General's huge bulk would build more than 50 three-bedroom houses. Among the last of their species, thousands of giant sequoias still remain in the park. Fortunately, they are reproducing themselves in logged-out areas at a rate that insures their survival for centuries if we continue to protect them.

Some of the stumps cut during the nineteenth century show rings dating back 3,000 or more years. Experts believe it is likely that some of the trees now standing were alive during the Bronze Age, 3,500 to 4,000 years ago. The longevity of the sequoia is due to several factors. For one thing its bark, which can be two feet thick, is unusually resistant to fire, insects, lightning, and disease. The trees also are exceedingly vigorous, outgrowing and dominating other species in the forest. Their only known weakness is a shallow root system that occasionally allows them to topple over without warning in a mild breeze.

No sequoia tree has ever been known to die of old age, but their existence is constantly threatened by their own shallow root systems that are seldom more than four feet deep.

dramatically down its eastern flank to Owens Valley. Viewed from the air, the Sierra Nevada resembles an immense ocean wave rolling east. Several major rivers rise within the drainage basins of these mountains, which contain country so remote that there are many places in the park where a backcountry hiker may not see another person for days at a time. There is one spot in the park that is said to be more distant from a road than any other location in the lower 48 states.

John Muir Trail runs through the park. This high-mountain walking route took 40 years to construct. From Yosemite it leads south for 218 miles across the snow-swept top of the High Sierra all the way to the flank of Mount Whitney. Dozens of supplementary trails connect with the Muir trail, giving hikers good access to the park's stunning alpine world of knife-edge ridges, glaciers, high mountain tarns, and meadows filled with wildflowers.

· ·

Sequoia-Kings Canyon National Parks

Established:	1890, 1940; Joint administration, 1943
Location:	California
When to go:	Open all year. (Winter access is limited.)
Size:	864,383 acres
Terrain:	Mountains, alpine valleys, canyons, and forests
Interesting sights:	General Sherman sequoia and Kings Canyon
Wildlife:	Bear, deer, bobcat, weasel, pine marten, wolverine, coyote, and mountain lion
Activities:	Ranger-led talks, walks, camera hikes, night-sky watches, children's programs, fire-fighting demonstrations, campfires, and snowshoe walks; fishing, bicycling, horseback trail rides, pack trips, downhill and cross-country skiing, and backpacking (by permit)
Services:	Three visitor centers, a nature center, four lodges, and 14 campgrounds
Information:	Three Rivers, California 93271; 209-565-3456

King of Canyons

The Kings Canyon area was first proposed as a national park by John Muir as early as 1891, the year after the creation of Sequoia National Park. But the park was not fully established until 1940. It bears the name of the river that in 1805 a Spanish explorer dubbed Rio de los Santos Reyes, or "river of the holy kings." Formation of this stunning steep-walled cleft in the granite of the Sierra Nevada began about 25 millions years ago as powerful geologic forces lifted up the land in what is now eastern California. About three million years ago, the highest peaks towered three miles above sea level. But then a series of earthquakes along fault lines in the earth deep below the Sierra Nevada cracked off the mountains' eastern face, which began sliding downward. This accounts for the stunning appearance of the eastern side of the mountains, which rises dramatically from Owens Valley.

Swiftly moving rivers made faster by gravity began carving narrow V-shaped canyons through the mountains. Over aeons the canyons plunged deeper into earth. During the Pleistocene ice ages, glaciers advanced into the Sierra Nevada and began scooping out basins that eventually became lakes and gouging out the walls of these canyons, making them sheer and steep. Nearly one and a half miles deep, Kings Canyon is the most dramatic of these glacier-carved defiles. Several other canyons in the park exceed 3,000 feet in depth, and Kern Canyon is nearly 6,000 feet deep.

The rush of water through granite has carved out the Center Basin of Kings Canyon. In this bleak place, grass and trees have gained only a tenuous foothold.

Channel Islands
American Galapagos

This elephant seal seems right at home on San Miguel even though this island has the harshest weather of any of the Channel Islands because it lies farthest west with no other islands to protect it.

Opposite: *Looking out across the sea from Anacapa, it is easy to imagine the submerged mountain chain whose peaks form the Channel Islands.*

Right: *Elephant seals like nothing better than a crowded beach, and once a seal has pulled itself up on the sand and wiggled slowly to a comfortable spot near another seal, it's likely to stay put for a long time.*

They rise up out of the mist on the horizon like distant mountains floating on a sea of clouds. The Channel Islands seem to be mystifying visions of a lost world across an elusive and undefined sea. The islands jut up from the Pacific Ocean near Santa Barbara in southern California. The eight offshore islands, five of which make up a unique national park, have always been especially intriguing. In the past access to them was limited. This gave them an air of mystery that was compounded by the fact that on some days the weather causes them to disappear altogether, only to rise out of the sea unexpectedly at a later time.

The four largest and northernmost islands, San Miguel, Santa Rosa, Santa Cruz, and Anacapa, are two to five miles apart. They are strung out like great peaks of a mountain range lost long ago to the relentless sea. It takes little imagination to picture their bases on the seafloor, surrounded by foothills and valleys. And this is exactly what the islands are. They are volcanic remnants of an ancient mountain range that was once the western extension of the Santa Monica Mountains, which extend eastward on the mainland from the Pacific coast. Today only the eroded peaks rise above the ocean, but the islands were formed by the same geologic upheaval that created the mountains on the mainland. About half a million years ago, violent and extensive earthquakes gradually separated the islands from the mainland, and over time wind and water eroded them down to the rocky outcroppings of today.

Always a sanctuary for unusual plants and animals, the islands were inhabited as early as 30,000 years ago by long gone people who left behind a cooking pit that still contains the burned bones of a small mammoth. How people or mammoths got to the islands remains a mystery. On Santa Cruz island, there are also remnants of kitchens and villages built by later inhabitants. More recently the Chumash lived here. They went to sea in long plank canoes, caulked with tar from oil seeps, to fish and to hunt for seals, whales, and sea otters. Their peaceful existence was shattered by the arrival of the Spanish explorer Juan Rodriguez Cabrillo, who landed on San Miguel island in 1542. The Spanish hired the native people to hunt sea otters for their pelts. Over time the Spanish brought other people to the islands to help with the hunt. They warred against the Chumash, finally driving them to the mainland.

Sea otters were hunted almost to extinction to satisfy the booming European fur business. Recently they have begun thriving again on the Channel Islands, which today are a refuge for wildlife and plants found nowhere else. Beaches, rocky harbors, and inlets provide a habitat for such exotic creatures as the northern elephant seal, which can weigh up to three tons and wriggles up sandy beaches on its belly. Thousands of California sea lions return to San Miguel each year to mate, give birth, and rear their young. Along with the sea otters, sea lions, and northern fur seals, the islands provide a home for thousands of nesting seabirds. A marine sanctuary extends for six nautical miles around each island, protecting a giant kelp forest that provides a habitat for nearly 1,000 species of fish and many unusual marine plants. Each December great gray whales stop by the islands to feed on the bountiful sea life.

Anacapa

Arch Rock rises 40 feet above the sea, hollowed out for aeons by wind and water. It makes a spectacular entrance to Anacapa island for visitors who have made the 90-minute journey by motor launch from the mainland. The formation was once part of the rocky island, but now it stands offshore as a dramatic, delicate arch.

After climbing up 154 steps from the landing platform, visitors can stroll along a one-and-a-half-mile nature trail on their own or join a park ranger for a guided tour that reveals a lot of island lore. In many ways Anacapa is a microcosm of the Channel Islands. Making a home here are such unusual plants as the tree sunflower, which bursts into a rich golden color in autumn. In spring and summer, thousands of wildflowers bloom here, despite the dearth of freshwater on the island. Elsewhere there are the remnants of a Chumash midden used for cooking. In spring thousands of sea birds, such as petrels and oystercatchers, nest on the island's rocky cliffs high above the sea. On fine days the nature trail offers outstanding views of the mainland from its vantage point on the cliffs more than 140 feet above the sea.

Channel Islands National Park

Established:	1980
Location:	California
When to go:	Open all year. (Access is subject to weather conditions.)
Size:	249,354 acres
Terrain:	Rocky islands with valleys, meadows, and dunes
Interesting sights:	Arch Rock and Anacapa
Wildlife:	Sea otter, seal, sea lion, pelican, numerous species of sea birds, hundreds of fish species, and gray whale (December through March)
Activities:	Ranger-led walks, evening programs, and wildlife and bird watching; tide-pool walks, swimming, snorkeling, scuba diving, fishing, hiking, whale-watching, and boat-in backcountry camping (by permit)
Services:	Three visitor centers (one on the mainland), three ranger stations, and three boat-in campsites
Information:	1901 Spinnaker Drive, Ventura, California 93001; 805-644-8262

Arch Rock, off Anacapa, rises 40 feet out of the sea. Wind and waves carved this dramatic entrance to the park from a huge piece of granite that was once part of the island.

Crater Lake
The Bluest Water

· ·

C rater Lake is a startling sight the first time you see it because of the intensity of its deep cobalt blue waters and the suddenness of its dramatic appearance. In much the same way that the area around the Grand Canyon does not prepare you for its magnificence, the terrain surrounding Crater Lake seems an unlikely location for such a large body of water. You approach the lake on a road that rises gradually through twists and turns up the side of a mountain clothed in forests of Shasta red fir, hemlock, and pine. Suddenly the road comes over a rise and plunges downward into a great basin, and there is the lake. At first you can hardly believe that you are seeing 25 square miles of water so blue that it looks like India Ink, circled by steep slopes, mountains, and great cliffs, which form a vast natural amphitheater.

Many of the park's features add to the spectacle of this remarkable lake. The Phantom Ship is an island made of lava with 160-foot-high ridges and peaks that resemble an ancient sailing ship. Discovery Point is the place where on June 12, 1853, a band of prospectors looking for gold first gazed on the lake. Hillman Peak is a 70,000-year-old volcanic cone, named for one of the prospectors, and Wizard Island is a volcanic cinder cone that rises about 700 feet above the lake's surface. Its name refers to the pointed hat worn by sorcerers, which it resembles, but there is also no doubt that there is plenty of magic in this stunningly beautiful place.

One of the lake's loveliest inlets, Steel Bay, was named in honor of William Gladstone Steel. He became intrigued by the lake from a newspaper article he read while he was still schoolboy. As an adult, Steel worked tirelessly to make Crater Lake a

In the eerie light of early morning as the sun glides over the rim of the crater, this lava island named Phantom Ship more than lives up to its name.

Opposite: *Wizard Island is a cinder cone that grew out of the crater after a blast, more than 6,800 years ago, created the enormous cave-in that later filled with water to become Crater Lake.*

Right: *Winter dominates the landscape of Crater Lake for much of the year. Each year's snowfall is about 50 inches, and some of it remains on the ground from December through April.*

· ·

national park. He lobbied for 17 years and appealed to President Theodore Roosevelt. Finally, in 1902, the nation's sixth national park was created, with the lake as its centerpiece.

The distance from the surface of the lake to its bottom is 1,900 feet, which makes it the deepest lake in the United States. Water has accumulated here over centuries as rain and snowmelt filled in a huge caldera. This vast bowl is the remnant of a volcano. Because no water flows into or out of the lake, its waters contain few minerals and almost no impurities. The lake's only fish, rainbow trout and kokanee salmon, were introduced by people.

Scientists today still do not fully understand the ecological character of the lake. Evidence of hydrothermal venting near the lake's bottom was discovered by manned submarines in 1989. This hot water may play an important role in the lake's ecology. Recently, green algae has been found growing at a record depth of 725 feet. This indicates to scientists that sunlight may penetrate deeper in Crater Lake than in any other body of water in the world. The lake's purity and its depth also account for its startling blue color.

The Pinnacles were sculpted by volcanic gases and erosion. First hot gases spewing out of tall vents solidified the rock; then erosion cut away the softer rock around the vents, leaving only the hardened spires.

Crater Lake National Park

Established:	1902
Location:	Oregon
When to go:	Open all year. (Winter access is limited.)
Size:	183,227 acres
Terrain:	Volcanic caldera, lake, forests, and unusual lava formations
Interesting sights:	Wizard Island and Phantom Ship
Wildlife:	Black bear, bobcat, deer, marmot, hawk, and eagle
Activities:	Ranger-led walks, children's and campfire programs, historical tours, and boat tours; hiking, bicycling, fishing, snowshoeing, cross-country skiing, and backpacking (by permit)
Services:	Two visitor centers, a park hotel, and two campgrounds
Information:	P.O. Box 7, Crater Lake, Oregon 97604; 503-594-2211

Creation of the Lake

How did a lake get on top of a mountain? Geologists believe the story begins long ago when a great 12,000-foot volcano, called Mount Mazama, formed as part of the chain of volcanoes in the Pacific Northwest that includes Mount Shasta and nearby Mount St. Helens. Legends repeated by native peoples that relate to quarreling between the deities of heaven and the netherworld have helped geologists construct a reasonably accurate timetable. The peak was built of lava flows, ash, and debris from repeated eruptions. About 4860 B.C., Mount Mazama erupted for the last time. This gigantic explosion catapulted volcanic ash and smoke miles into the air. After the blast Mazama's peak remained as a shell over a hollow interior. Apparently the ancestors of the native people who knew the legend of Mazama watched the summit finally collapse with a deafening roar. This geologic event created a huge smoldering caldera. After rain and snowmelt filled the basin, forests of hemlock, pine, and fir and meadows of wildflowers began to grow in the lava and ash on the rim of the caldera. Soon bobcats, deer, marmots, bears, hawks, and eagles arrived to make this place their home.

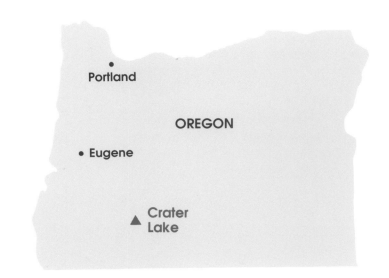

Wizard Island rises about 800 feet from the surface of the lake. Its red rocks and extremely sparse vegetation are evidence of relatively recent volcanic activity.

Mount Rainier
Icy Heights

Fed primarily by snowmelt, voluminous Comet Falls on Van Trump Creek plummets 320 feet over a series of steep rock terraces.

Opposite: *From late July through August, lupines, Lewis monkeyflowers, asters, meadow parsley, Sitka valerian, and a host of other wildflowers offer a lush contrast to snowy mountain peaks.*

Right: *The glacier-clad, 14,410-foot summit of Mount Rainier pokes through the clouds, staying high above the storm that is flooding the volcano's flanks with a sudden downpour.*

On a clear day, you can see the snow-capped summit of Mount Rainier from more than 100 miles away. It is one of the world's largest volcanoes, and at nearly three miles in height, it is the tallest peak in the Cascades. Rainier simply overwhelms the surrounding 6,000-foot mountains that look like courtiers paying homage to a monarch. The mountain often seems to float alone among the clouds, and when you see it from a great distance, its enormous height, compared with the neighboring peaks, makes it appear closer than it is. In the evenings, as the sun begins dropping below the Pacific horizon, the last light bathes the great mountain's summit, washing it in a warm pink glow that lasts long after darkness has come to the lowlands.

Even though the mountain is obviously its most important feature, the park has many other attractions. Below the great snow fields and glaciers on the upper flanks of Mount Rainier are spectacular fields of wildflowers that burst into bloom in late spring and summer. As the snow melts, an astonishing array of color marches up the slopes. Here you will see a profusion of monkeyflowers, buttercups, avalanche lilies, Indian paintbrush, asters, and lupines, rushing to bloom during the brief respite from the cold that often ends during the final week of August.

Where there are not meadows, there are great forests, some with trees that are more than 1,000 years old. The woods provide a home for countless birds and animals, such as tiny chickadees, lumbering black bears, and curious golden-mantled ground squirrels that look like chipmunks without their stripes. Higher up on the slopes, mountain goats forage for food on ridges blown free of snow. Here too, finches nest in the rocks

in summer and feed on heather buds and high-altitude insects, while hoary marmots and tiny pikas hoard dried grass for winter food.

Mount Rainier was forged by fire and shaped by ice. Most geologists believe its birth occurred less than a million years ago on a mass of solidified lava left by earlier volcanoes. New upswellings of lava, ash, and pumice (lava formed with trapped bubbles of gas) poured from the young volcano's vent thousands of times. Gradually, layer upon layer of debris piled up, forming a summit cone about 16,000 feet high. Scientists used to think that about 1,500 feet was missing from the top of the peak because it had been destroyed in a great eruption. But today they believe the missing summit was lost in a huge mud flow that took place about 5,000 years ago. Even without its original top, Mount Rainier is one of America's great peaks and the dominant volcano of the Cascade Range. When naturalist John Muir wrote about the mountain, he stated what many people who have seen it feel: "Of all the fire mountains which, like beacons, once blazed along the Pacific coast, Mount Rainier is the noblest."

· ·

Mount Rainier National Park

Established:	1899
Location:	Washington
When to go:	Open all year. (Winter access is limited.)
Size:	235,404 acres
Terrain:	Volcanic peak, foothills, valleys, and canyons
Interesting sight:	Emmons Glacier
Wildlife:	Black bear, deer, mountain goat, marmot, pika, finch, small mammals, and birds
Activities:	Ranger-led nature and history walks, hikes, campfire and children's programs, talks, and films; mountain climbing, hiking, fishing, cross-country skiing, snowshoeing, and backpacking (by permit)
Services:	Three visitor centers, a hiker information center, two park inns, and five campgrounds
Information:	Tahoma Woods, Star Route, Ashford, Washington 98304; 206-569-2211

Climbing Rainier

More than 10 percent of the surface of Mount Rainier National Park is permanently covered by ice. Even as eruption after volcanic eruption built the mountain, glaciers from the Pleistocene ice ages were carving valleys and canyons on the mountain's slopes. Today 25 major glaciers remain. This is the largest collection of permanent ice on a single mountain in the United States south of Alaska. Emmons Glacier is at a lower elevation than any other glacier in the nation.

Austere and serene, the summit of Mount Rainier draws mountain climbers of every age and ability from around the globe. The ascent takes two days, with most of the first day taken up by a long hike through the forests and rocky slopes of the mountain's lower two-thirds. The second-day trip to the top crosses the weathered surface of a moving glacier, one of six that drops down from the summit. Using ice axes, crampons, and steel spikes fixed to their boots, climbers make their way between deep crevasses that have fragmented the ice into fissures and canyons. In some places they cross crevasses on bridges of unmelted snow.

The top of the mountain is a small crater left by the most recent eruption a little more than a century ago. Climbers usually walk around the crater to the Columbia Crest. At 14,410 feet this is the highest point on the peak, and from this vantage point on fine days you have an unsurpassed view of the Pacific Northwest.

· ·

· Seattle   Spokane ·

WASHINGTON

Mount
Rainier ▲

Vancouver
·

Viewed from the height of the Tatoosh Range, Reflection Lake does not catch the image of Mount Rainier. Instead the pristine tarn reflects the intense blue of the bright sky.

North Cascades
Alpine Wonderland

· · · · · · · · · · · · · · · · · · · ·

Cascading water and fine mists transform bare rocks into a glistening intricate design.

Opposite: *Diablo Lake fills the bottom of the Skagit River valley, which was carved out thousands of years ago by mile-thick glaciers whose heirs still cling to the tops of some of the Cascade Mountains.*

Right: *Forbidden Peak more than lives up to its threatening name: Its rocky, treacherous rim is protected by several large glaciers.*

This is a land of mountains and a land of ice. More than 300 glaciers are concentrated in North Cascades National Park. There are many more glaciers here than can be found anywhere else in the United States south of Alaska. The looming presence of mountains also defines this park. Here you will find great soaring, glacier-scoured peaks, spires that pierce the clouds, ragged ridges, alpine tarns, and flower-bedazzled meadows in cirques below the mountain summits. On the flanks of the mountains, forests of fir and pine surround tranquil lakes and deep glacial valleys.

North Cascades is also a land of special sounds. On warm days you hear the booming crack of sloughing ice and the thunderous roar of avalanches. When the weather is bad, thunder blasts up the valleys and circles the peaks, while the wind rushes between the mountains and ridges, and down the slopes of glaciers. At all times there is the background sound of falling water in this mountain range that was named for its innumerable cascading waterfalls.

The peaks of the North Cascades are so rugged and vertical that these mountains are often called the American Alps. Like the European Alps, the vast wildness of the park draws scores of mountaineers, hikers, and backpackers. In 1814 trapper Alexander Ross wrote of this jagged terrain: "A more difficult route to travel never fell to man's lot." The names of some of the mountains in the region attest to the hardships they imposed on early trappers and prospectors: Damnation Peak, Mount Despair, Mount Fury, Forbidden Peak, and Desolation Peak.

· · · · · · · · · · · · · · · · · · · ·

The glaciers that carved wide valleys through the Cascades have retreated to the mountaintops where they continue to soften the contours of these rough young mountains.

North Cascades is a topographic jumble, consisting of two national park units (North and South) as well as two national recreation areas (Ross Lake, named for the early trapper, and Lake Chelan). All four are administered by the National Park Service. A road through the Ross Lake area, which was completed in 1972, divides the North and South units and makes the alpine wonderland of the park readily accessible.

The mountains themselves create another kind of division within the park. Moist prevailing winds blow in from Puget Sound and the Strait of Juan de Fuca. Flowing up the western slopes and cooling as they rise, the moist winds condense into rain and snow. The west side of the park is covered by lush green forests of Douglas fir, western red cedar, and hemlock, which grow to towering heights because the trees receive more than 100 inches of pre-cipitation a year. By contrast the western slope of the mountains, lying in the rain shadow of the great peaks, re-ceives on average only a little more than 30 inches of precipitation a year. Douglas firs on the west side of the mountains reach only half the height of firs on the eastern slope. Moisture-loving hemlocks do not grow here at all; instead the western slopes foster trees that tolerate dryness, such as ponderosa and other pine trees.

North Cascades National Park

Established:	1968
Location:	Washington
When to go:	Open all year. (Winter access is limited.)
Size:	684,000 acres
Terrain:	Rugged mountains, valleys, and lakes
Interesting sights:	Stehekin Valley and Cascade Pass
Wildlife:	Black bear, mule and black-tailed deer, mountain lion, bobcat, marmot, pika, finch, small mammals, and birds
Activities:	Ranger-led nature walks, talks, and campfire programs; hiking, boating, fishing, hunting (in season, by special permit), horseback riding, rafting, cross-country skiing, and backpacking (by permit)
Services:	Two visitor centers, an information center, a ranger station, and seven campgrounds
Information:	2105 Highway 20, Sedro Woolley, Washington 98284; 206-856-5700

Cascade Pass

There is only one paved road that runs all the way through the park, the North Cascades Highway. As the road climbs higher and higher, the landscape changes from alder forests to huge groves of towering Douglas firs, then to forests of pine, larch, and hemlock, and finally, flowering alpine meadows and a high windy pass. From this point hikers can set off on an old trail to 5,384-foot Cascade Pass atop a ridge covered with alpine meadows, which in summer are painted with wildflowers.

In the high meadows black-tailed and mule deer graze; black bears look for huckleberries, which they rake into their mouths, vine and all, with their claws; and stout marmots sunbathe on rocks. Some lucky visitors catch a glimpse of mountain goats clambering on high rocky crags. They rely on soft cupped pads on their hoofs to give them their incredible traction. Throughout the park roam bobcats, which you will seldom see, and secretive mountain lions. Sleek and tawny, these big cats prey on deer and other mammals, helping to keep the wildlife population in balance.

Looking up from a creek bed below Cascade Pass, the stark, icy summit of Magic Mountain looms over towering Douglas firs and moisture-loving hemlocks, which prosper on the west side of the Cascades.

Olympic
Three Parks in One

As soon as spring melts the snow on Hurricane Ridge, wildflowers burst forth in a profusion of color that lingers through the short summer.

Opposite: *Only the muted sound of almost-perpetual rainfall disrupts the peaceful quiet of the Hoh Rain Forest, where soft mosses, gentle ferns, and giant trees muffle a silent world.*

Right: *The Pacific Ocean relentlessly pounds the headlands of the Olympic mainland, quickly eating away the soil and then eroding the rocks that only temporarily project out of the sea.*

Come to Olympic and you enter an enchanted forest, a luminous world suffused with a soft green light reflected and refracted by trees garlanded with club moss and lush growths of ferns and oxalis. Here, in the Hoh Rain Forest, western hemlock, Sitka spruce, and western red cedars, some with diameters of 25 feet, tower 300 feet above you. These ancient giants, standing on enormous roots, called stilts, form great colonnades with inviting, winding side aisles that look like green tunnels leading to another world.

A jumble of undergrowth spreads out far below the forest canopy in the national park on the Olympic Peninsula, located in the extreme northwest corner of Washington. Seedlings that would have been unable to compete with other plants on the forest floor sprout exuberantly on fallen trees, called nurse logs. From these rotting logs, some saplings may grow into the world's largest specimens of Douglas fir and western hemlock. The undergrowth is luxuriant and abundant, but it is not impenetrable because its growth is kept in check by the foraging of the park's most famous inhabitant, the Roosevelt elk.

Olympic is the most diverse national park. Along with the Hoh and two other rain forests, the park contains two more equally distinct ecosystems: a rugged wilderness seacoast, with stunning headlands and lovely beaches covered with driftwood, and the Olympic Mountains, a rugged range of high alpine meadows, great jagged ridges, and glaciers. Because of this remarkably diverse landscape, climatic changes within the park are unbelievably abrupt. The western side of the park has the wettest weather in the United States, averaging nearly 12 feet of precipitation each year. The eastern side of the park, which lies in the rain shadow of the mountains, is the driest area on the Pacific coast north of Los Angeles.

In 1788 an English sea captain, named John Mears, sighted the peninsula's tallest mountain, which at 7,965 feet is not an extremely high peak, but it rises so dramatically above the sea that it looks enormous. Mears was so overwhelmed by the sight that he named the peak Mount Olympus in honor of the home of the Greek gods. In the 1890s area residents tried to block a proposal for federal protection of thousands of acres of timber that would restrict the area's huge logging industry. But since 1897 the territory has been under the jurisdiction of either the Department of Interior or the Department of Agriculture. For 24 years it was Mount Olympus National Monument, but the name was changed when the national park was established in 1938.

The heart of the park is the Olympic Mountains, a wilderness range that is nearly circular. The mountains are penetrated by 13 rivers that radiate out from their center like the spokes of a wheel. The highlands are up-and-down country, where the peaks and ridges are separated by deep valleys and canyons cut by the rivers. Geologists believe that the rock of the mountains developed beneath the sea because marine fossils are found near the summits. About 30 million years ago, the great plate carrying the floor of the Pacific Ocean collided with the North American plate. The upper levels of the seabed plate rose up and crumpled into the Olympic Mountains. Later glaciers, wind, and water shaped the mountains into what we see today: breathtaking vistas of deep canyons, towering mountain ridges, and meadows dense with wildflowers.

Life of the Rain Forest

Olympic's three rain forests, with trees and vegetation as lush as an Amazon jungle, may be the strangest and most fascinating sections of this unusual park. The richness of these forests exists only because certain conditions are met: Moisture must be incredibly plentiful, and even when it is not raining, the air needs to be humid and misty. And the temperature must be mild, neither too hot nor too cold.

The nearness of the Pacific Ocean helps fulfill these requirements for the Olympic forests. The steep rise of the inland mountains forces Pacific storm clouds to ascend and release their moisture as heavy rainfall. This moisture is then concentrated in long river valleys, which also extend moderate, sea-level temperatures deep inland. This unique combination of weather and topographical conditions perpetuates the life cycle of these forests: After a tree falls, it can become a nurse log for new seedlings. Bacteria and fungi slowly break down the fibers of the fallen log, which becomes covered by mosses and lichens. This surface is rich in nutrients and allows seeds to germinate and sprout. After a seedling takes root, a young sapling grows. Over time the nurse log rots completely away, leaving a tree standing tall on its stiltlike roots.

Olympic National Park

Established:	1938
Location:	Washington
When to go:	Open all year
Size:	922,000 acres
Terrain:	Coastal wilderness, rain forest, and mountains
Interesting sights:	Hoh Rain Forest and Mount Olympus
Wildlife:	Roosevelt elk, snowshoe hare, Douglas squirrel, Olympic marmot, pocket gopher, Beardslee trout, small mammals, and hundreds of species of birds
Activities:	Ranger-led walks and campfire programs; hiking, boating, fishing, climbing, swimming, windsurfing, waterskiing, river rafting, cross-country and downhill skiing, and backpacking (by permit)
Services:	Two visitor centers, a museum, information stations, and 15 campgrounds
Information:	600 E. Park Avenue, Port Angeles, Washington 98362; 206-452-4501

Several kinds of moss clothe a bigleaf maple with a thick cloak of intense green that almost overwhelms the tree's own foliage.

Haleakala
House of the Sun

· ·

A great mountain, Haleakala, lies sleeping on the Hawaiian island of Maui. This volcano is a wild moonscape that extends for 33 miles in one direction and 24 miles in the other. In one direction its slopes drop sharply away to the sea, and in the other direction the distant peaks of Mauna Loa and Mauna Kea are visible on the neighboring island of Hawaii. The top of this great mountain is a 19-square-mile circular crater. Its floor, which is 2,720 feet below the summit, is a starkly beautiful and forbidding landscape of cinder cones and sculptures of lava colored startling shades red and yellow. Haleakala is a volcano that has grown cold, but its enormous crater is filled with unearthly shapes and profiles that are vivid reminders of its fiery past.

Light from the sun comes early to the rim of the vast crater, and it remains here long after darkness has fallen on the lower slopes of the mountain. Haleakala means "house of the Sun," and according to legend, the mischievous demigod Maui tamed the sun in the great mountain's summit basin. Long ago there were only a few hours of light each day because the Sun was so lazy that it hurried home at night to rest. The demigod's mother was unable to dry her clothes during the few hours of sunshine, so Maui climbed to the mountain's summit where he caught the Sun by trapping its first rays as they crept over the crater's rim at dawn. He released the Sun only after it promised to move more slowly across the sky.

Haleakala has not had a major eruption since about 1790, according to both Hawaiian legend and records kept by Europeans. Maps and charts made by early European explorers show significant changes in the island's topography that

These cinder cones formed in the crater of Haleakala during a second period of volcanic activity that was even more intense than the explosive days of the volcano's creation.

Opposite: *This high volcanic desert vibrates with color released by the effects of weather on lava that turns gray iron particles to bright red, adds a touch of yellow from sulphur, and brings out the sparkle in once-buried crystals.*

Right: *The name Haleakala (pronounced: holly-ah-ka-lah) means "house of the Sun," from the legend of the demigod Maui holding the Sun captive in the volcano's crater.*

· ·

American writer Mark Twain once told a friend that if he ever needed to get away from it all, he would shut himself "up in the healing solitudes of the crater of Haleakala and get a good rest."

• •

probably resulted from the flow of lava. But even though Haleakala is dormant, nobody would call it extinct. Earthquakes on Maui indicate to geologists that the great volcano still rumbles far below the surface, and islanders adamantly believe the sleeping mountain will wake up breathing fire again within a century. Haleakala's gigantic crater was not created by the kind of explosion that blew the top off Mount St. Helens in 1980. After thousands of eruptions built up the mountain from the bottom of the Pacific Ocean, a climatic change brought long-lasting torrential rains. Water flowing down the sides of the peak turned into huge rivers pouring from the summit. These raging streams cut long, deep valleys down the flanks of the mountain. The crater was created as two of the valleys joined at the mountaintop and eventually eroded it into the vast amphitheater.

Today the mountain's crater, which really is not a crater but a canyon, is a dry, desolate terrain where it can be unbearably hot during the day and frosty cold at night. The bowl is pocked with small craters and studded with cones formed of cinder and ash. Puu O Maui, the tallest of these

Formation of a Pacific Volcano

For centuries Hawaiian legends have explained the way in which volcanic islands form. Pele, the goddess of fire, moves from place to place around the islands. As she tells others the story of her travels, she stamps her foot, making the earth tremble and forming a new island.

Geologists know that there is some truth to this legend. The spot where an island is likely to appear does move from place to place. Scientists explain this with a theory of "hot spots" and plate tectonics. For some unknown reason, there are about 100 hot spots beneath the earth's surface. These places produce more molten rock, or magma, than is produced elsewhere. The Hawaiian hot spot is one of the largest.

The hot spots are stationary, but the dozen or so great plates that make up the crust of the earth are not. The Pacific plate is in constant motion at the rate of about four inches a year. As the plate moves over the Hawaiian hot spot, enough magma rises to create a new island. This young island is pulled away from the hot spot by the movement of the plate, and in time another island forms over the hot spot.

There are no roads within the crater, but thirty miles of trails lead visitors through the desolate terrain, which is relieved somewhat by moisture from fog and rain on its eastern side.

multicolored figures, rises 600 feet above the stark topography. A landscape that is more inhospitable to plants and animals would be hard to imagine, but in one corner, where a break in the crater wall allows moisture to seep in on waves of clouds, leather ferns, called 'ama'u, thrive along with other unusual plants. In other places you will find silversword, an endemic plant with dagger-shaped leaves that grow out in silky, symmetrical balls. This rare plant takes four to 20 years to grow to maturity, sends out a single, magnificent flower stalk in a burst of summertime bloom, then withers and dies.

Although the crater is the centerpiece of the park and its major attraction, Haleakala also has regions of coastline and mountain desert. The park has been designated a United Nations International Biosphere Reserve. The road to Haleakala's summit rises from close to sea level to over 10,000 feet in just 38 miles. It is believed to be the steepest route for automobiles in the world. The ascent passes through a number of climatic and vegetation zones. Lower down it is humid and tropical; a little higher the terrain becomes subalpine. Here mamane, a yellow-flowering brush, brightens the slopes and small birds are everywhere. If you are lucky, you might see some of Haleakala's famous honeycreepers. These brightly colored birds are believed to be descended from the first birds other than seabirds ever to reach Hawaii. Since their arrival, they have evolved into at least 47 species.

From the eastern summit of the crater, the park's other major attraction, the rain-forested Kipahula Valley, drops thousands of feet in a great sweeping curve down to the coast. The upper valley is a protected wilderness that is home to a profusion of animals and plants, some among the world's rarest, as well as an array of insects found nowhere else on earth.

Haleakala is sacred to the Hawaiians, and the remains of ancient stone structures within the crater indicate that religious ceremonies were held here more than a thousand years ago.

209

Silversword grows nowhere else in the world except on this mountain. When the plant matures, after as long as 20 years of growth, it bursts into dazzling deep-red blooms only once and then it dies.

Haleakala National Park

Established:	1960
Location:	Hawaii
When to go:	Open all year
Size:	28,655 acres
Terrain:	Volcanic mountain and rain forest
Interesting sights:	Haleakala Crater and Kipahulu Valley
Wildlife:	Nene (Hawaiian goose), honeycreeper, parrotbill, and hundreds of other bird species
Activities:	Ranger-led walks and talks; hiking, horseback riding, swimming, and backpacking (by permit)
Services:	Visitor center, three cabins in the crater, and two campgrounds
Information:	P.O. Box 369, Makawao, Maui, Hawaii 96768; 808-572-9306

Visiting Kipahulu Valley

The lush Kipahulu Valley begins at a narrow piece of parkland on the southeastern coast of Maui. This coastal area was farmed more than 1,000 years ago, and throughout the valley, you can see archaeological remains of stone walls, temples, and shelters. This is a primal landscape dominated by green forests, meadows, and cascading waterfalls. The gorge of the 'Ohe'o Stream cuts through this section of the valley. This defile is filled with picturesque pools, with water cascading from one to the other. Until the 1920s sugarcane was grown along both sides of the `Ohe`o Stream, and wild cane still grows in patches.

From the gorge the Pipiwai Trail leads to the lovely Makahiku Falls, which is more than 180 feet high, and then on to a double waterfall. Along the trail you can pick mango and guava fruit. Higher still, through a luxuriant forest that includes a dense stand of bamboo, which clatters mysteriously in the wind, you arrive at your destination, the Waimoku Falls. Drawing visitors for centuries, this solemn cascade, 300 feet high, fills a jungle clearing with mist and the perpetual sound of falling water.

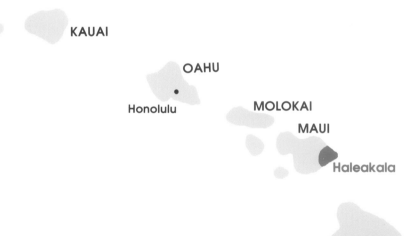

East of the summit of Haleakala, the dense tropical rain forest, lush with ferns and flowering tress, rings with the bright sound of falling water from high Wailua Falls and countless other waterfalls.

Hawaii Volcanoes
Fire from Below

• •

The amazing phenomenon featured in this national park begins as a deep rumble, more felt than heard. Sometimes this reverberation is coupled with an ominous, slow hiss that sounds like a disturbed snake. A series of temblors may follow: slow rumbling quakes or great cracking snaps in the ground. These early warnings may last for hours or days. Suddenly a fissure opens, and as it lengthens rapidly, it emits a blast of steam followed by a fiery fountain of white-hot lava that shoots hundreds of feet into the sky. More and more spouts of lava burst from fresh cracks, and at night they light up the sky for miles around. The frightening roar builds to an overwhelming cascade of sound, and the acrid smell of sulfur is everywhere.

It is impossible to witness such a spectacle and not realize that the most colossal raw powers of nature are on display. There are few better places to see this grandest of all sound-and-light shows than on the Big Island of Hawaii at Hawaii Volcanoes National Park. There are five volcanoes on the island, two of which are encompassed by the park: Mauna Loa and Kilauea. They are among the world's most active volcanoes. More than 4,000 feet above sea level and still growing, Kilauea rises from the southeastern flank of the older and much larger Mauna Loa.

These fiery mountains are not huge steep-sided cones topped with snow, like Fuji-san in Japan or Mount Rainier in Washington. Instead, these volcanoes in Hawaii rise more gently from the sea to a great caldera on the summit. This kind of mountain is called a "shield volcano" because the top looks like an ancient

Pahoehoe is the Hawaiian name for the plump ropes of lava that flow from eruptions of Kilauea.

Opposite: *The spectacular display of Pu'u O eruptions is rarely dangerous to people. The volcano gives plenty of warning, which scientists can now readily interpret, before it begins spewing lava.*

Right: *Halemaumau is the crater atop Kilauea. It is the legendary home of the goddess Pele and a place that scientists have determined is a lava pipeline to the earth's surface from its molten interior.*

• •

warrior's shield lying face down. Mauna Loa, which means "long mountain," rises 13,677 feet above the Pacific Ocean. It is second in height on Hawaii only to Mauna Kea, a quieter volcano. The elevation of Mauna Loa can be topped by many mountains, but its actual size is astonishing. Measured from its base, which is 18,000 feet below the surface of the Pacific, Mauna Loa exceeds Mount Everest by 2,000 feet in height. Its volume of more than 10,000 cubic miles, making it the world's most massive single mountain. Its bulk is about 100 times that of Mount Rainier. Atop Mauna Loa a large caldera, called Mokuaweoweo, contains several summit craters that have erupted in the past, covering much of the caldera floor with lava twisted into nightmarish shapes, great pits, and cinder cones.

Eruptions within the craters of both of the park's volcanoes are relatively harmless. The outbursts give good advance notice, and because they are fascinating and exciting to watch, an impending eruption draws thousands of people to the crater's rim. More dangerous eruptions break out through huge fissures in the flanks of the mountains as underground pressures mount, forcing lava from the openings. Flowing slowly like a great, hot tidal wave down the slopes, an advancing wall of lava can destroy crops and whole villages in its path. Despite this awesome power for destruction, which is rarely dangerous to human life, Hawaiians have always cherished and respected their awesome mountains. Ever since the first people arrived here about 1,500 years ago in huge double-hulled, ocean-going canoes, Hawaiians have woven fascinating and enchanting legends about the great gods and goddesses who inhabit the volcanoes and causes them to erupt.

Kilauea Summit

Often called the "drive-in volcano" because its summit is so accessible, Kilauea has an awesome caldera two miles across and three miles long that is surrounded by ragged, barren cliffs hundreds of feet high. Inside this vast bowl, fantastic lava shapes cover miles of barren landscape that looks like a desert on another world. Most of the time, the caldera emits wisps of steam. In its southern end, there is a great fiery pit that is 3,000 feet across and over 200 feet deep. This volcanic crater is called Halemaumau, or "fern house."

Up until 1924 the crater contained a lake of molten lava that bubbled constantly. More recently the crater has been the scene of some of nature's most spectacular fireworks as wild fountains of fire spray upwards, while lava flows from great fissures in the floor. According to legend, this is the home of Pele, the goddess of fire. Geologists confirm that this may be the earth's major opening for the upward flow of lava.

Hawaii Volcanoes National Park

Established:	1961
Location:	Hawaii
When to go:	Open all year
Size:	229,177 acres
Terrain:	Volcanic mountains, desert, and forest
Interesting sight:	Kilauea crater
Wildlife:	Honeycreeper, Kipuka Puaula, and hundreds of bird species
Activities:	Ranger-led, walks, talks, slide shows, and films; hiking, backcountry fishing, art center, workshops, seminars, and backpacking
Services:	Visitor center, a museum, three campgrounds, a hotel, and cabins
Information:	Hawaii 96718; 808-967-7311

KAUAI

OAHU

Honolulu

MOLOKAI

MAUI

HAWAII . Hilo

Hawaii Volcanoes

This spray of lava looks like fire, but it is not flaming. The orange glow is the lava itself, which is about 2,000 degrees Fahrenheit when it comes out of the earth.

American Samoa
Pacific Wonderland

A merica's newest national park is about 5,000 miles southwest of Los Angeles, about 2,500 miles south of Honolulu, and closer to Auckland, New Zealand, than it is to any city in the United States. Samoa is a dazzling chain of jewellike islands twinkling across a lonely expanse of the South Pacific. Five of the easternmost islands and two sparkling coral reefs comprise American Samoa National Park. Formed by volcanic activity originating on the floor of the ocean, the islands are a tropical paradise of mountains, rain forests, deep harbors, and stunning white beaches.

The national park preserves tropical rain forests, coral reefs, and an endangered 4,000-year-old culture. Tutuila, the largest island of American Samoa, is crowned with two great volcanic peaks rising above steaming rain forests. A great natural harbor nearly cuts the island in two. At its head lies fabled Pago Pago, sometimes called Pangopango, a South Seas island village that is American Samoa's capital and only port of call. The northern and most accessible section of the park rises above Pago Pago's harbor in great volcanic ridges covered with dozen upon dozens of species of tropical trees and vegetation. The park encompasses coastal villages, tropical lagoons, and a dramatic scenic highway with fine views of a Pacific coral reef. Among the unusual wildlife found here are hundreds of brightly colored birds as well as the endangered flying fox, which is a bat with the wingspan of an eagle.

The beaches on the island of Ofu are spectacularly beautiful, and offshore a vibrant coral reef shelters large numbers of brightly colored tropical fish.

Opposite: *Looking across Afono Bay, Polo island juts out of the ocean—a worn volcanic peak that will eventually succumb to the erosive action of wind and wave.*

Right: *Each year between 200 and 300 inches of rain pour down on the mountains of American Samoa, nourishing dense tropical rain forests that are the home of enormous fruit bats, called flying foxes.*

217

The largest section of the park, about 5,000 acres, lies on Ta'u, the easternmost island and a half-hour flight from Pago Pago. This section includes Lata Mountain, which seems to rise nearly straight up from the Pacific, and at 3,170 feet is the highest volcano in the islands. The Ta'u section of the park also includes 300 offshore acres. The park's smallest section is on Ofu, a volcanic island just west of Ta'u. It encompasses only 260 acres of land and water, but the area is one of the finest beaches in the South Pacific. Most people agree that this stretch of white sand and stately palms defines what a tropical paradise should look like. Lying just offshore and protecting a lovely blue lagoon, a healthy coral reef teems with a vast array of sea life.

For more than 4,000 years, members of Polynesia's oldest culture have lived on these islands. Samoa means "sacred earth," and the name reflects the belief of the people that the islands are a special place to be cherished and protected. In 1988, believing that their own ancient culture also needed protection, Samoan chiefs agreed to lease some of their territory to a national park. Permanent leasing arrangements are still being worked out, and visitors require permission to enter this new and unusual park.

American Samoa National Park

Established:	1988
Location:	American Samoa
When to go:	Open all year. (Permission is required to enter.)
Size:	About 8,870 acres
Terrain:	Volcanic islands, tropical rain forests, beaches, and coral reefs
Interesting sights:	Lata Mountain, rain forests, and coral reefs
Wildlife:	Hundreds of tropical bird species and flying fox
Activities:	Tours, swimming, and walking
Services:	All visitor facilities are currently located outside the park.
Information:	American Samoa Office of Tourism, P.O. Box 1147, Pago Pago, American Samoa 96799; 011-684-699-9280

OFU

American Samoa

TÁ

Pago Pago

TUTUILA

Formation of a Coral Reef

Visitors to American Samoa National Park have an opportunity to see firsthand some of the best preserved coral reefs in the Pacific Ocean. The reefs harbor an astonishing array of sea life: vibrantly colored fish in hundreds of varieties dart around the spectacular limestone formations that protect them from the vagaries of the weather, strong Pacific currents, and such predators as the several species of sharks that haunt the reefs.

Coral reefs are produced over centuries by the secretions of colonies of tiny polyps, usually stony corals. The accumulation of their skeletal material is gradually broken and piled up by the motion of the waves. The structure of the reefs changes constantly although this is not evident to the casual observer. There are three kinds of coral reefs: the barrier reef, which usually lies far offshore and protects a wide deep lagoon, such as Australia's Great Barrier Reef; the atoll, a reef surrounding a lagoon with no central island; and the fringing reef, a coral platform close to the shore that follows the coastline, such as the reef found in American Samoa National Park.

Endangered sea turtles nest safely on the beaches of Ta'u. Electric lights on some other Pacific islands disorient the turtles so that they are now often unable to find their traditional nesting grounds.

The view from Mount Alava reveals the intense blue of South Pacific waters framed by the lush green of a dense coastal forest.

Katmai
The Smoking Valley

· ·

Streams flowing down from encircling mountains have carved this stark valley, filled with ash and pumice to depths of hundreds of feet, into deep and spectacular gorges. One sheer-walled canyon, hewed by the serpentine Ukak River, is crowned by cliffs of volcanic ash that in places are 400 feet high. Although a few plants have been able to gain a tenuous foothold here and there, the valley is essentially lifeless, a moonscape of desolation that looks as if it had recently suffered a terrible catastrophe. The great cataclysm occurred in 1912 when a volcano erupted here on the Alaska peninsula with a force that geologists believe was 10 times greater than the explosion that took the top off Mount St. Helens in 1980. The eruption was heard hundreds of miles away as a new volcano formed and an older one collapsed. For hundreds of miles up and down the coast, the daylight sky was darkened by thousands of tons of ash thrown more than 30,000 feet into the sky. Global temperatures cooled for weeks, and as far away as Vancouver, British Columbia, acid rain burned up clothing that was hanging out to dry. It is believed that nobody witnessed the actual eruptions, because it occurred in a wild and uninhabited region far from towns or villages. But the great eruption put Katmai on the front pages and sparked interest in the region.

In 1915 and 1916, botanist Robert Griggs led expeditions into the area to find out exactly what had happened. As he climbed up on top of Katmai Pass, he could scarcely believe his eyes: "The whole valley . . . was full of hundreds, no thousands—literally, tens of thousands—of smokes curling up from its fissured floor." He named the place the Valley of Ten Thousand Smokes. Today the smokes, which were fumaroles that sent jets of steam as high as 1,000 feet in the air, are gone. But the place is nearly as bleak

With a powerful leap, a salmon pushes itself up Brooks Falls on its way to spawn. For at least 4,500 years, people have lived near this river and harvested the rich crop of salmon.

Opposite: *When Mount Katmai collapsed in on itself during the eruption in 1912, it created the basin for this lake, which was still boiling when botanist Robert Griggs visited the area in 1916.*

Right: *The Ukak River slices its way through a wasteland of 45-foot-deep of volcanic ash in the Valley of Ten Thousand Smokes.*

· ·

221

The Bears of Katmai

Brown bears, the continent's largest land carnivores, have made the Katmai area their home since the most recent Pleistocene ice age. Averaging 1,000 pounds in weight and measuring up to 10 feet long, the bears spend the long Alaskan winter in dens they have excavated in hillsides or under exposed tree roots. Not true hibernators, they sleep fitfully off and on, sometimes waking up enough to wander around outside in the snow.

They wake up for good in early spring (April in Katmai), poke their heads outside, and lumber out to find food. If the bear is a female, there is a good chance that she has birthed a pair of cubs during the winter. Visitors to the park delight in the marvelous and often amusing antics of these clumsy youngsters fishing for the first time. Bear watching in the park is best in midsummer, the spawning season of sockeye salmon, which are the meal of choice for these bears. Sometimes they dive completely under the water of a fast-moving river to catch fish, while at other times they dexterously catch jumping fish in midair.

as it was on the day that Griggs first set foot in the valley, which is now the centerpiece of Katmai National Park. The valley is almost totally barren, and it is crossed by only a few streams and trails. One of these trails leads 3,800 feet up an icy, ashy slope to the rim of Mount Katmai. When you look down into the caldera from here you can see a lake the color of a robin's egg.

Another highlight of the park is Novarupta, a 200-foot dome of volcanic rock believed to be the extrusion plug of the 1912 eruption. Geologists believe that most of the lava and ash from the eruption was emitted here and that magma was drawn away from nearby Mount Katmai, which collapsed as a result.

Beyond the Valley of Ten Thousand Smokes, Katmai is a wilderness wonderland of mountains, rivers, and forested valleys. Sitting atop an especially hot section of the Pacific Rim of Fire, the park contains 15 active volcanoes, many still emitting steam from open vents and fissures. Along with its volcanoes, the park's other main attraction is North America's largest population of brown bears. About 750 of the protected animals roam through the park's huge backcountry areas. One of the best places to see these magnificent creatures is from a viewing platform overlooking Brooks Falls, a half mile from the Brooks Camp Visitor Center. Here, nearly every day in spring and summer, you can witness the marvelous spectacle of the great bears skillfully catching fish for dinner.

Katmai National Park

Established:	1980
Location:	Alaska
When to go:	June to mid-September
Size:	4,090,000 acres
Terrain:	Forested valleys, streams, mountains, and volcanic terrain
Interesting sights:	Bears at Brooks Falls and the Valley of Ten Thousand Smokes
Wildlife:	Brown bear, moose, wolverine, small mammals, and birds
Activities:	Ranger-led walks, talks, evening programs, and bus trips to the Valley of Ten Thousand Smokes; bear-watching, hiking, kayaking, canoeing, boating, mountain climbing, aerial sightseeing, fishing, float trips, and backpacking
Services:	Visitor center, three lodges, cabins, a wilderness retreat, and a backcountry campground
Information:	P.O. Box 7, King Salmon, Alaska 99613; 907-246-3305

This Alaskan brown bear can afford to bide his time and wait for an easy catch because each year more than a million salmon come to the waters of Katmai to spawn.

Lake Clark
Quintessential Alaska

E xcitement for the trip across Cook Inlet from Anchorage to Lake Clark National Park begins even before visitors board their aircraft for the one-hour flight. On some clear days, smoke can be seen billowing in puffs from one or both of the park's two active volcanoes, Iliamna and Redoubt. More and more white-mantled mountains loom up as your plane approaches the park. Suddenly you are flying through Lake Clark Pass, and before you spreads out what looks like an endless enchanted wilderness: Rugged mountains with gleaming blue glaciers flowing down through the valleys between them, winding rivers, waterfalls cascading hundreds of feet to end in multicolored sprays of foam, and the flanks of mountains covered with blazing red and orange fireweed. As you fly out of the pass, the great lake where you will land appears.

Lake Clark is about 50 miles long and five miles wide, and its color is a lovely blue. On its southeastern shore, the little community of Port Alsworth is the site of the park's field headquarters and the place where most visitors settle in for a good long look at some of North America's most outstanding and varied scenery. All of Alaska seems to converge here. The backbone of the park is the Chigmit Mountains, a range as rugged as mountains can get; they appear to rise directly from great sheets of ice. These peaks are the spectacular meeting place of the Alaska Range that dips down from the north and the Aleutian Range that rises up from the south. To the west of the jagged Chigmit Mountains is the great Turqoise-Telequana Plateau, a wilderness preserve for herds of wandering caribou. The tundra here is similar to Alaska's North Slope. Black bears wander the mountains along with Dall sheep, at their southern-most limits here. Alaska's state tree, the Sitka spruce, is at its

With the coming of dawn, the pristine reflections of neighboring 6,000-foot peaks begin to show themselves on the mirror surface of Turquoise Lake.

Opposite: *The tundra on the foothills and around the shores of Turquoise Lake is visited annually by 20,000 caribou in the Mulchatna herd. Here they forage and bear their young.*

Right: *Lake Clark is nearly 50 miles long and five miles wide. At dusk the lake exchanges its characteristic light blue color, which is created by glacial debris in the water, for the more muted tones of evening.*

northernmost limit in the park. Throughout the valleys, there are dense conifer forests.

The park also has three rivers, the Mulchatna, Tlikakila, and Chilikadrotna, that have been officially designated Wild and Scenic. In this strictly fly-in park with no roads, canoeing or kayaking these and other rivers is the only way to get close to this magnificent wilderness. The park's rivers and lakes also offer some of the finest fishing in the world, with Dolly Varden trout, northern pike, and five kinds of salmon (chum, king, coho, humpback, and sockeye).

Connecting the southwestern end of Lake Clark to Iliamna Lake, the Newhalen River is an excellent place to watch the annual migration of salmon upriver to spawn. This river is as clear as fine crystal, making it possible to see the salmon from an airplane. During the spawning season, which begins in late June, the fish arrive at the Alaska coast after traveling thousands of miles through the Pacific. In peak years the migrating salmon color the river red. As many as nine million fish fight their way upstream to Lake Clark and its shallow tributaries where they themselves were spawned.

Flowing between jagged unnamed peaks in the interior of the Chigmit Mountains, this glacier continues on its course, pulled forward by gravity over its base of ice pellets.

ALASKA

Fairbanks

Lake Clark

Anchorage

Lake Clark National Park

Established:	1980
Location:	Alaska
When to go:	Summer
Size:	4,045,000 acres
Terrain:	Mountains, lakes, valleys, coastline, and tundra
Interesting sights:	Lake Clark Pass and salmon migrating on the Newhalen River
Wildlife:	Moose, black bear, Dall sheep, Arctic grayling fish, salmon, wolverine, small mammals, and dozens of seabirds
Activities:	Kayaking, rafting, boating, fishing, backpacking, mountain climbing, bird and wildlife watching, aerial sightseeing, and hunting (by permit)
Information:	4230 University Drive, Suite 311, Anchorage, Alaska 99508; 907-271-3751

Exploring Lake Clark

L ake Clark is a park where wilderness reigns supreme, a land of glaciers, volcanoes, alpine peaks, and costal inlets, with countless seabirds, herds of caribou, and great roving bears. Lake Clark is a dazzling place to explore. Access to most areas of the park is by water, either air taxi, boat, or kayak. Taking a kayak out on Lake Clark itself is an open invitation to wander where you will, exploring its many inlets and miles of coastline. The smaller lakes in the park also offer excellent kayaking, while some of the rivers give experienced kayakers or rafters fine white-water experiences.

Surprisingly, the opportunities for organized hiking in this great wilderness park are somewhat limited. The only maintained hiking trail is just two miles long. Beginning in Port Alsworth on the shore of Lake Clark, the trail leads through a forest of birch and black spruce, around bogs and ponds, and along the shore of the rough-and-tumbling Tanalian River. You will see moose in the ponds, Arctic grayling fish in the river, Dall sheep on the slopes of Tanalian Mountain, and bears practically everywhere. Elsewhere in the park, there are good but less well marked hikes around the shores of lakes, between lakes, and into the rugged mountains.

Above Lake Clark the soft and springy tundra is overrun with twiggy white caribou lichen that resembles miniature staghorns and adds a touch of winter white to the subtle tapestry of colors.

Kobuk Valley
Land of Shifting Sands

· · · · · · · · · · · · · · · · · · ·

The Kobuk is not the largest river in Alaska, but in the Eskimo language the name means "great river" because ever since people came to live in this place the Kobuk has been an important source of food and the main east-west route.

Opposite: *There are several places in this 25-square-mile area of constantly moving sand that date back 24,000 years.*

Right: *Each autumn the caribou arrive here at Onion Portage in scattered bands to join the large herd that will head south to spend the winter in the subarctic forests.*

The Kobuk Valley is pure arctic terrain. Its wide bowl is filled with great boreal forests and tundra that creeps up the lower slopes of the mountains. Flowing from its headwaters in the Brooks Range on the east and draining into the Hotham Inlet, the Kobuk River glides across the heart of the valley. Its floor is so flat that the river drops only about two or three inches every mile. The river's barely detectable current makes it look like a lake in places where it is especially broad.

The river is the main artery for transportation in Kobuk Valley National Park, which lies entirely above the Arctic Circle and has no roads. A paddle or motor trip on the river usually begins from the little settlement of Ambler on the east side of the park and ends in Kiana, a village outside the park's western boundary. Floating on the river, you will find solitude in the wilderness. Kobuk Valley is the least visited of all national parks. In 1989 there were fewer than 1,000 visitors to this remote natural realm where Eskimos still hunt the great herds of caribou that migrate through the area each summer.

Placid and pleasant, the Kobuk River flows through land belonging to the Inupiaq Eskimos. In places steep banks rise above the water, while elsewhere great boreal forests line both shores, interrupted by lakes and tundra. In late August and early September, you can sit above the river and watch huge herds of caribou swim across the river, the great antlers of the males bobbing and swaying with the motion of the water. In a stream that meanders through a grassy meadow down to a confluence with the river, you are likely to see a grizzly bear fishing for dinner, its enormous paws slashing through the water with lightning speed.

· · · · · · · · · · · · · · · · · · ·

South of a bend in the river on the eastern side of the park, great sand dunes appear suddenly. This is an arctic Sahara in a strange and unlikely setting. East of the dunes is Onion Portage, the park's best known feature, which is named for the wild chives that grow here. For thousands of years, migrating caribou have splashed across the river here on their way south for the winter. Here too, evidence indicates that hunters have waited for them. In 1961, at Onion Portage, archaeologist J. Louis Giddings found what has been called the most important archaeological site in the Arctic. Giddings uncovered a two-acre site that yielded layers of flint-working technology, representing seven different cultures dating back at least 10,000 years. The site, now inactive and overgrown, provides important clues to the puzzle of the human migration across a land bridge from Asia to North America.

Kobuk's Moving Dunes

Sand is everywhere, shifting and blowing with the wind and the weather. It stretches for 25 square miles south of the Kobuk River. In this barren landscape, summer temperatures can reach 100 degrees Fahrenheit. These rolling active hills, colored yellow and beige, are more than 24,000 years old. Geologists believe they came into existence long before the last ice age, about 10,000 years ago, when the Kobuk Valley was an ice-free refuge with grassy tundra similar to that found spreading across Siberia today.

The great dunes, along with a smaller five-square-mile tract farther east, were formed by the weathered and wind-blown debris left by an earlier ice age. An unusual combination of geology, topography, and prevailing winds keeps the dunes on the go. Generally inhospitable to vegetation, the dunes of Kobuk Valley are advancing at the rate of about an inch a year through a doomed boreal forest that is in their path. Visitors to the park reach the dunes by boat and can take a short walk through the sand.

Kobuk Valley National Park

Established:	1980
Location:	Alaska
When to go:	Open all year. (Summer is the most accessible season.)
Size:	1,750,421 acres
Terrain:	Arctic valley, rivers, lakes, and sand dunes
Interesting sights:	Great Kobuk Sand Dunes and Onion Portage
Wildlife:	Caribou, brown bear, small mammals, and birds
Activities:	Rafting, kayaking, canoeing, hiking, fishing, aerial sightseeing, and backpacking
Services:	Backcountry camping
Information:	P.O. Box 1029, Kotzebue, Alaska 99752; 907-442-3573

At their western edge, the Great Kobuk Sand Dunes encroach on the surrounding spruce forests. The dunes are the windblown outwash of melting glaciers.

People have come to Onion Portage to hunt caribou for at least 10,000 years, leaving behind artifacts from seven separate and distinct cultures.

Glacier Bay
The Power of Ice

S cientists think of Glacier Bay, Alaska's southernmost national park, as a living laboratory, where they can study the natural processes that occur during the retreat of a glacier. The ice here is moving back from the sea at a spectacular rate; it is the fastest glacial retreat on record. In 1794, when British sea captain George Vancouver sailed up the Alaska coast, Glacier Bay did not exist. Vancouver saw only a great wall of ice, several miles wide and thousands of feet thick. In the intervening two centuries, the ice has receded more than 65 miles, leaving in its wake a spectacular fjord-rimmed bay, surrounded by forested mountains that only now are returning to life following a long hibernation.

At the southern end of the bay, where the ice first departed, the land is now covered with a lush rain forest of spruce and hemlock. Looking today as though it had been there forever, the forest of great trees, rising from a spongy moss floor, has been able to sustain rampant growth because of moisture-bearing winds from the Pacific that supply year-round precipitation. Farther north, in areas of the bay more recently deglaciated, the vegetation is sparser and the terrain more rugged. At its head the bay branches into two great arms, Muir Inlet and West Arm. They in turn are feathered by numerous small inlets. Alder and willow forests today grow on slopes that were covered by glaciers only 50 years ago. But at the heads of the small inlets, glaciers still calve icebergs, which drop into the water with the roar of distant cannon. This sound is called "white thunder" by the Tlingit Indians.

There are 16 tidewater glaciers that flow down from the mountains to the sea at Glacier Bay. Most of the glaciers in the park's eastern and southwestern ends are receding at rapid

The glaciers are pulling back from the land at the rate of about one and a half feet a year. This Sitka spruce, thickly hung with moss, grows on land that was under the ice 200 years ago.

Opposite: *From Muir Inlet the view toward the Fairweather Range spans more than 50 miles, but the huge mountains seem deceptively closer than they actually are.*

Right: *When John Muir built a cabin in this inlet, which bears his name, he picked a site at the foot of the glacier. If it were still standing, the cabin would now be 20 miles from Muir Glacier.*

rates, but some glaciers on the west side are advancing. Scientists believe the depth of the water in the inlets, which affects air temperature, plays the crucial role in determining whether a glacier retreats or advances.

Here in the land of gleaming blue ice, ground that has been laid bare for only two or three decades is already starting to nourish new, although sparse, vegetation. Mosses, lichens, and mountain avens can survive on bare rock, and yellow dryad, a low-growing plant with lovely red-and-yellow flowers, can live in the sand and gravel left by melting ice. This diversity of emerging plant life creates a habitat for wolves, mountain goats, moose, black and brown bears, and an array of smaller wildlife. The bay, which is as recently uncovered as the land, supports a food chain that begins with microscopic algae, which provide food for krill. These tiny shrimplike sea creatures are themselves fed on by the soaring fish populations. Harbor seals, with a penchant for basking in the sun on small icebergs, and harbor porpoises, nourished by the abundant sea life, make the bay their home for part of the year. At the top of the food chain are killer whales; they feed on fish and harbor seals.

The park's largest visitors, humpback whales, which are as long as 50 feet and weigh more than 40 tons, arrive each summer to cruise the waters for the tiny krill that are the mainstay of their diet. Today the great bay is a source of endless activity both on- and offshore. This environment is less than two centuries old, but it provides spectacular and fascinating viewing for human visitors.

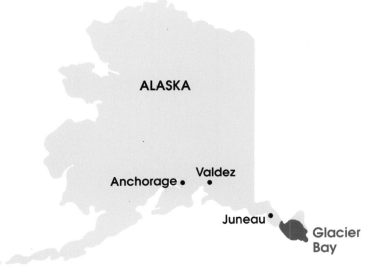
ALASKA

Anchorage ●   ● Valdez

Juneau ●   ● Glacier Bay

Glaciers and Icebergs

The 16 glaciers that wind their way down the valleys of Glacier Bay National Park like tremendous white highways were formed during climatic periods when more snow fell during the winter than melted and evaporated in summer. As snow builds up in layers winter after winter, its own vastly increasing weight causes the snow to compact into small grainy pellets that become crystals of ice. Eventually this level of ice reaches such a great depth and weight that it begins to move downhill in the direction dictated by gravity. The compacted ice crystals deep beneath the surface function like frozen ball bearings, gliding over one another and enabling the entire mass of ice to slide. As one of these glaciers inches its way into the waters of Glacier Bay, fissures that have developed in the ice along with the rough motion of the sea causes huge chunks to break away, or calve, with a resounding crack that can be heard miles and miles away.

Glacier Bay National Park

Established:	1980
Location:	Alaska
When to go:	Late-May to mid-September
Size:	3,283,168 acres
Terrain:	Bay, fjords, glaciers, and mountains
Interesting sight:	Muir Inlet
Wildlife:	Moose, wolf, black and brown bear, ptarmigan, bald eagle, salmon, harbor seal, harbor porpoise, killer and humpback whale
Activities:	Ranger-led walks, films, slide shows, and evening programs; kayaking, fishing, boat tours, glacier viewing, whale and birdwatching, hiking, mountain climbing, cross-country skiing, aerial sightseeing, and backpacking
Services:	Two information centers, a park lodge, and one campground
Information:	Gustavus, Alaska 99826; 907-697-2230

Margerie Glacier is a thick jumble of ice that corkscrews down from the Fairweather Range for more than 20 miles to Tarr Inlet, where its sheer ice cliffs rise 180 feet above the water.

Wrangell-
St. Elias
Awesome Wilderness

. . . .

The glacier-fed Chitina River cuts back on itself in so many places that it has created a charming series of small forested islands along about half its length.

Opposite: *Mount Drum is an old, cold 12,010-foot-high volcano that never sheds its thick mantle of ice and snow even when summer has melted the unnamed lake at its base.*

Right: *Icy Bay in the Gulf of Alaska is the birthplace of many icebergs, which break off from the glaciers that extend down from the Bagley Ice Field.*

In a land of great mountains and glaciers that go on for hundreds and hundreds of miles and wilderness so untamed that thousands of acres are still untrodden by people, Wrangell-St. Elias stands out for the sheer audacity of its topography. Three great mountain ranges converge in the park, creating a reckless jumble of ragged peaks, lovely and wild river valleys, and enormous glaciers. The St. Elias Mountains, the world's tallest coastal range, shove their way up from the Yukon Territory in the southeast where in a torrent of glaciers and ice fields they join the Chugach Range. The mighty Wrangell Range, coming down from the north, is the backbone of the park.

Near the point where the three ranges come together, in the southeast corner of the park, spectacular Mount St. Elias rises 18,008 feet. It is the second tallest mountain in the United States. (Mount McKinley is the tallest.) Only 30 miles from the rugged, glacier-scoured coast of the Gulf of Alaska, Mount St. Elias rises so dramatically and precipitously that it dominates its surroundings like few other mountains. Elsewhere in the park are eight more of the 16 tallest peaks in the United States; four of them are above 16,000 feet. As you fly over the park, the mountains come at you in waves of ranges that change color with the weather.

Floating on a raft down one of the park's many rivers, you will see Dall sheep on the tundra and mountain goats on the rocky crags of mountain slopes. But there are so many huge glaciers in this park that there is not very much habitable terrain. The park's largest glacier, Malaspina, is so big that Rhode Island could fit on it. This rugged region has been called the Himalayas of North America. In fact, the rugged terrain of the park may actually be

. . . .

wilder than the great Asian mountains. There are still valleys in these mighty Alaskan mountains where people probably have never set foot, and countless peaks remain unnamed and unscaled. The park is so vast that it contains more unexplored terrain than the Himalayas, largely as a result of the short summers and long winters that come with its proximity to the Arctic.

The park's size is overwhelming: The biggest national park by far, it is larger than Switzerland and six times the size of Yellowstone. But it is not inaccessible. Two roads lead into the heart of the park. The road from the Chitina River Valley goes to two tiny towns that are remnants of the gold and copper mining frenzy at the turn of the century. Today each of these small communities has fewer than a dozen residents. They are staging areas for hiking, rafting, climbing, and kayaking adventures in the park.

• •

Wrangell-St. Elias National Park

Established:	1980
Location:	Alaska
When to go:	Summer
Size:	13,188,000 acres
Terrain:	Mountains, glaciers, and valleys
Interesting sight:	Kennicott town site
Wildlife:	Dall sheep, mountain goat, bear, wolf, moose, boreal owl, osprey, salmon, small mammals, and birds
Activities:	Horseback ricing, pack trips, river running, kayaking, lake fishing, mountain climbing, hiking, aerial sightseeing, and backpacking
Services:	Visitor center, three ranger and information stations outside park boundaries, two private campgrounds, three lodges, and one bed and breakfast
Information:	P.O. Box 29, Glennallen, Alaska 99588; 907-822-5234

Visiting Alaska's Past

One of Wrangell-St. Elias's two good unpaved roads leads visitors back in time to the Alaska gold rush days at the turn of the century. From the ranger station at Chitina on the east side of the park, the road follows the abandoned Copper River and Northwest Railroad for 62 miles to its end. There a hand-pulled cable tram takes you across the Kennicott River to the tiny community of McCarthy. Now almost deserted, it was once a town of 2,000 miners, hustlers, and card sharks.

From the McCarthy side of the river, where you can rent a bicycle or hire a taxi, another dirt road leads to the ghost town of Kennicott, the site of a 13-story mill that was abandoned in 1938. The mill and other deserted buildings here are covered with ferrous-oxide red paint and trimmed in white. They are among Alaska's finest and most photogenic samples of turn-of-the-century structures. The copper mine at Kennicott, which is now on the National Register of Historic Places, was once the world's richest.

ALASKA

Fairbanks

Wrangell-St. Elias

Anchorage •

Valdez •

• Juneau

The Chitina River flows out of the St. Elias Mountains and meanders along a braided course between the Chugach and Wrangell mountains on its way to join the Copper River.

The imposing peaks of the Wrangell Mountains seem to touch the clouds when they are viewed from the Chitina-McCarthy road, which follows a railroad bed that was originally built to bring ore out of the Kinnecott mining region.

Kenai Fjords
Mountains and Ice

• •

The Harding Ice Field, which is nearly 700 square miles of frozen grandeur that is as much as a mile thick, crowns the mountains of Kenai Fjords in south-central Alaska. This is a raw, ragged land that has not yet recovered from the great Pleistocene ice sheets that flowed over most of Alaska 12,000 years ago. The rocks of the coast here are so jagged, sharp, and uneroded that land and sea seem to be locked in a fearsome struggle for dominance: The sea challenges the land with deep, lovely fjords and hundreds of inlets and coves while the coast, for its part, abuts into the relentlessly crashing surf of the Gulf of Alaska with great, rocky headlands and clawlike peninsulas that seem to be struggling to survive in the pounding water.

Kenai Fjords encompasses the essence of Alaska's southern coast. The park contains wild, powerful ice; dynamic geology; spectacular mountains with great glaciers flowing down between them to the sea; and awesome fjords that provide a wild habitat for thousands of nesting seabirds and seafaring mammals. The land has a rough, unfinished look to it, and remnants of the last ice age are still at work here. A vast torrent of wild whiteness, the enormous Harding Ice Field feeds more than 30 glaciers that reach out from it and down through the mountains like great tentacles. This glistening field of seemingly endless ice is covered here and there by great drifting dunes of snow that move constantly with the vagaries of the wind. In places the peaks of mountains buried by the ice since the Pleistocene Era rise above the icy plain. In stormy weather, these peaks, called nunataks, seem to float like castles on a sea of white. They are awesome reminders of an age, not so long ago, when vast sections of the world were cold, frozen, and lifeless.

The Harding Ice Field is now only 35 miles long by 20 miles wide, but the protruding mountain tops, called nunataks, were deeply scared by the even larger ice field that once covered them.

Opposite: *Nature is constantly reshaping the coast of Kenai. Today a coastline lowered by an earthquake in the 1960s and higher tides are lengthening and deepening the fjords.*

Right: *At Three Hole Point in Aialik Bay, the steady pounding of the surf has battered a series of arched openings in a steep islet.*

• •

A humpback whale quietly slips to the surface of the water, paying no attention to the incredible scenery of sea stacks, glaciers, and the peaks of the Kenai Range.

Exploring Kenai Fjords

The inlets, coves, fjords, islands, and even glaciers of Kenai Fjords offer hikers and boaters many opportunities for exploring and seeing wildlife in a spectacular natural setting. The barren Chiswell Islands, serviced by ferry boat, are an excellent place to see giant Steller sea lions, basking, playing, and fighting on the rocks. Females, which give birth to pups in June, may weigh as much as 600 pounds, while the bulls can weigh more than a ton.

McCarty Fjord in the southern end of the park slices deeply into the mainland for 23 miles with great cliffs towering nearly a mile above the water. Here and in adjacent Nuka Bay is a fascinating array of terrain, including a 900-foot waterfall and historic gold mining camps. Along the shores you are likely to see black bears, moose, martens, and river otters, while in the icy inlets protruding into the landscape from the sea you might see a humpback whale jumping almost completely out of the water in a dramatic display of power and joy.

ALASKA

Anchorage

Kenai Fjords **Juneau**

Kodiak

Vast as it seems today, the Harding Ice Field is a relatively small remnant of the much larger ice cap that once covered the entire region. As the ancient ice advanced, then retreated, then advanced again over the centuries, it carved out the rugged coastline of the Kenai Peninsula and gouged out the fjords. Finally, as the earth's climate warmed, the ice began melting, leaving in its wake a spectacular landscape and habitats for throngs of wildlife.

At least 20 species of seabirds nest by the thousands on the rocky crags of the fjords. Clown-faced puffins make their homes among the rocks. These stubby birds with short wings fly only with difficulty, but they are as graceful underwater, when diving for fish, as they are ungainly in the air. Peregrine falcons hunt for small mammals on the rocky islands that dot the coastline, while bald eagles soar among the cliffs of the fjords. Black bear and wolverine, along with moose and lynx, roam a narrow zone of lush rain forest between the coast and the icy mountainsides, which is home to mountain goats that climb on rocks so exposed they would give pause to an experienced mountaineer.

Kenai Fjords National Park

Established:	1980
Location:	Alaska
When to go:	Open all year. (Winter access is limited.)
Size:	670,000 acres
Terrain:	Mountains, glaciers, coast, fjords, and islands
Interesting sight:	Harding Ice Field
Wildlife:	Moose, black bear, wolverine, marten, lynx, mountain goat, bald eagle, peregrine falcon, puffin, harbor seal, northern sea lion, sea otter, and humpback whale
Activities:	Ranger-led hikes to glaciers and ice field, and evening campfire programs; mountain climbing, sailing, camping, fishing, kayaking, aerial sightseeing, boat trips, cross-country skiing, dogsledding, snowshoeing, and backpacking
Services:	Visitor Center, ranger station, two cabins, and one campground
Information:	P.O. Box 1727, Seward, Alaska 99664; 907-224-3874

Glacier-fed cascades hurdle thunderously down the side of Storm Mountain toward the fjord below.

Gates of the Arctic
The Awesome North

• • • • • • • • • • • • • • • • • • • •

Some people believe that Gates of the Arctic National Park in northern Alaska is a perfect example of true American wilderness. It is a place so pure and lovely that it is the same today as it was long before people ever set feet here. Climb almost any ridge in the park, and you will find yourself gazing upon range after range of unbelievably jagged peaks that slice into a sky filled with brooding clouds. Separated by these serrated mountains are lovely forested valleys cut by meandering rivers. This is a haunting, timeless land, where you feel deeply the call of nature and know the possibility that the valley beyond the next ridge is a place where no person has ever walked before. The park lies entirely above the Arctic Circle and includes the heart of the awesome Brooks Range, one of the world's most northern mountain systems. Six hundred miles long, the great range was a mighty barrier to travel until construction of the oil pipeline and the accompanying Dalton Highway.

The vast territory of this park, the second largest national park and the farthest north, embraces parts of two very different worlds. The southern slopes of the mountains are covered with scraggly black spruce forests, called taiga, which is Russian for "land of little sticks." These spunky trees struggle for survival in river valleys at the earth's northernmost limit for trees. From the northern flanks of the mountains spread mile after mile of treeless arctic tundra. This is a vast region of startling and unexpected contrasts. For nine months of the year, the great arctic plain is one of the most hostile places on earth. The wind

Amid the dark beauty of this unnamed hidden valley of the Killik River on the north slope of the Brooks Range, any evidence of animal or human life seems misplaced.

Opposite: *Because its peaks are absolutely barren and remain polished with snow even in August, the Brooks Range seems to be a lot taller than its 7,500 feet.*

Right: *On a hike up the Koyukuk River, Bob Marshall, the founder of the Wilderness Society, encountered two then-nameless peaks, which to him appeared to be the Gates of the Arctic.*

• •

blows incessantly and the temperature often drops to 80 degrees below zero Fahrenheit in the perpetual night of an arctic winter. Then suddenly in mid-June, with the sun above the horizon for 24 hours each day, the tundra comes alive with wildflowers. Almost everywhere grasses and sedges, along with white reindeer moss, carpet the tundra. Dwarf willows grow in jumbles where the ground is soggy from the melting snow of the late arctic spring.

This profusion of plants supports a remarkable variety of animal life and great herds of caribou. Along with Kobuk Valley National Park and the Noatuk National Preserve between the two parks, Gates of the Arctic preserves much of the habitat of the western arctic caribou. These large deer with magnificent antlers spend their summers on the tundra, where they bear their young. With the coming of winter, the caribou migrate in herds, numbering in the thousands, over time-worn passes through the Brooks Range to feeding grounds hundreds of miles to the south. Also roaming the severe landscape in search of food are brown bears, wolves, ferocious little wolverines, and foxes.

The mountains of the Brooks Range are awesome black granite crests with sharp overhangs and glacier-honed vanes. No trees grow here, and the lichens that are beginning to green the valley may take 150 years to reach their full growth.

Exploring Gates of the Arctic

The park takes its name from conservationist Robert Marshall who visited the area in the early 1930s. Hiking through the valley of the North Fork of the Koyukuk River in June, a month when sunlight keeps the wild land ablaze with a bright red light until 2 a.m., Marshall came upon a pair of unusually steep mountains, one on each side of the river. He called the peaks Gates of the Arctic: "No sight or sound or smell or feeling even remotely hinted of men or their creations. It seemed as if time had dropped away a million years and we were back in a primordial world."

Today visitors to the park find it as primitive as ever, a place where it is still possible to sit beneath a tree that never before sheltered a human. Although hiking is a rewarding experience in the alpine regions of the park, rivers that have been followed for centuries by Eskimos and caribou still provide the major travel routes through Gates of the Arctic. Six designated Wild and Scenic Rivers cascade out of high alpine valleys into forested lowlands where they become more manageable streams. Alatna River has given many visitors a stunning tour of the park. The river runs gently down from the treeless Arctic Divide in the northwest corner of the park through lovely tundra to a confluence with the Koyukuk River in a spectacular forested valley.

Gates of the Arctic National Park

Established:	1980
Location:	Alaska
When to go:	Summer
Size:	8,500,000 acres
Terrain:	Mountains, valleys, and arctic tundra
Interesting sight:	Gates of the Arctic
Wildlife:	Caribou, brown bear, wolf, wolverine, fox, ptarmigan, snowy owl, small mammals, and birds
Activities:	Hiking, backpacking, canoeing, kayaking, rafting, fishing, hunting (with license), mountain climbing, and birdwatching
Services:	One lodge
Information:	P.O. Box 74680, Fairbanks, Alaska 99707; 907-456-0281

In spring melting snow turns the tundra into a spongy carpet of grasses and sedges, punctuated with ponds and pools.

Denali
The Great One

● ● ● ● ● ● ● ● ● ● ● ● ● ● ● ● ● ● ●

T his park and the entire wild, rugged region that surrounds it pay homage to a single geological entity: Mount McKinley, or Denali, "the Great One" as native Alaskans call it. At 20,320 feet above sea level, this magnificent mountain is North America's highest peak, and one of the grand mountains of the world. Denali's sheer bulk and the immense rise of its perpetually white-mantled summit above its surroundings make it look like a monument left by ancient gods in the depths of a distant time. In terms of height from base to summit, McKinley is the biggest mountain in the world. Its awesome north face rises 18,000 feet from a 2,000-foot subarctic plateau to its peak. Like the Grand Canyon, Denali is one of the great spectacles of the American landscape, a sight that once seen will never be forgotten.

When the clouds cooperate, which occurs only about half the time in summer, Mount McKinley presents an overpowering spectacle anytime during the day or long summer night. At midday the great peak sparkles as the bright sun glints off the snow and glaciers that cover its flanks from bottom to top. At sunrise or during the long subarctic twilight, the great mountain is almost beyond belief. It becomes a magnificent mass of granite, ice, and snow enshrouded in delicate pastel shades of pink, mauve, and purple, which change with the slow movement of the sun. The shifting light makes the mountain look deceptively soft and ethereal.

The park that encompasses the mountain and its surrounding peaks in the Alaska Range is a huge wilderness tapestry that is larger than the state of Connecticut. The mountains here, unlike the Rockies and the Sierra Nevada, are not covered with forests, because in northern latitudes the timberline falls between 2,000

The pale snow that always enshrouds Mount McKinley is echoed by the almost colorless surface of Wonder Lake as it picks up the soft light of a late-summer dawn.

Opposite: *Resplendent in the bright northern sun, Mount McKinley is the proud crown of the continent, rising 20,320 above sea level and still growing.*

Right: *Lichens spread slowly over soil that has been buried by snow for thousands of years, gradually returning fertility to the lifeless terrain.*

● ● ● ● ● ● ● ● ● ● ● ● ● ● ● ● ● ● ●

and 3,000 feet instead of 11,000 to 12,000 feet. This means that most of the park is treeless. It is a broad open landscape that creates a feeling of vastness which can be overwhelming.

There are two worlds of Denali: the raw alpine region of the high mountains and the tundra-covered lowlands. Connecting one to the other are the great glaciers that flow down from the summits of McKinley and the other peaks. For decades the main travel route into the mountains has been the Muldrow Glacier, an immense river of ice fed by three tributaries: the Harper, Brooks, and Traleika glaciers. Each originates in cirques (glacier-gouged rock basins) high on the mountain.

The ice that becomes the Muldrow begins just below the peak's summit and flows northeastward 35 miles through a granite gorge on the side of the mountain to its leading edge, or snout. On the tundra far below the summit the ice melts, feeding the McKinley River. Twice in the past century the glacier, for reasons not fully understood, has surged forward. The last time was during the winter of 1956-57 when the Muldrow's snout suddenly advanced five miles across the tundra. Its movement was accompanied by the constant and alarming sound of breaking, grinding ice and the rush of water. Despite the debris and jumbled ice left by the Muldrow's last leap forward, the glacier is still used as a major climbing route up the mountain.

Denali was the first national park to be established in Alaska, and it was originally called Mount McKinley. The park was renamed in 1980, the same year the other seven national parks in the state were established by the Alaska Lands Act. Together the eight Alaskan parks contain a staggering 41 and a half million acres, more than all the other national parks combined. Alaska's most popular park, Denali, seems unusually civilized and accessible compared with other Alaskan parks, especially Kobuk Valley and Gates of the Arctic. The Anchorage-Fairbanks highway leads directly to Riley Creek Information Center on the park's eastern border, and the Alaska Railroad has a passenger station here. From this eastern gateway, a gravel road leads deep into the park's subarctic landscape.

Exploring Denali

In a park as vast as this, the opportunities for exploring are practically endless. Most visitors begin by taking the park bus on the 85-mile gravel road that extends deep into the Denali wilderness. From the visitor center on the eastern boundary of the park, the bus climbs out of a stunted spruce forest onto the treeless tundra that rolls through valleys and over gentle ridges to the flanks of Mount McKinley.

Offering stunning vistas of the Alaska Range along the way, the road winds along Primrose Ridge and then drops into marshy flats and through the so-called "drunken forest" of spruce trees that lean every which way. The trees slant because of the ground's yearly freezing and thawing cycles. After crossing three passes, the road finally reaches the Eielson Visitor Center at mile 66, a rest stop frequented by ground squirrels and even an occasional grizzly. After passing within a mile of the great snout of the Muldrow Glacier, the road comes to its terminus at the Wonder Lake Campground. From here the view is magnificent. If the weather cooperates you can see the sheer Wickersham Wall, McKinley's north face, which rises for more than 14,000 feet and is one of the most awesome mountain walls in the world.

This caribou bull sports a new rack of antlers that is still covered with soft dark velvet, which will soon fall off in strips unless the impatient bull rubs off the itchy coating on the rough bark of a tree.

For eight months the land around the great mountain is shrouded in snow, but June brings weather warm enough to initiate a brief growing season that greens the lower elevations.

Despite these relative amenities, wildlife is so visible and abundant here that Denali has been called a "subarctic Serengeti." There are shy wolves, vicious little wolverines, lumbering moose, and quick foxes, as well as countless birds and small mammals, such as the tiny pikas that inhabit the slopes of the great peaks. Grizzly bears are the undisputed sovereigns of this wild terrain. They roam the park at will. The great bears, which require as many as 100 square miles to support each one, feed mainly on roots, berries, and other plants. When they are ravenously hungry after a winter's hibernation, the bears also go after arctic ground squirrels, injured caribou, or moose calves.

On a summer day, with up to 24 hours of daylight, visitors to Denali see sights they will remember for the rest of their lives. A huge herd of caribou migrate through a pass below Mount McKinley toward their summer feeding grounds in the north. On a green meadow on Primrose Ridge, a band of two-dozen pure-white Dall sheep pause briefly as they make their way to the high alpine crags where they spend their summers. A golden eagle soars off a cliff along Polychrome Pass on the park road, while a moose wades in ankle-deep water, bathed in the warm colors of the day's end. The eerie call of a loon rolls across Wonder Lake. Maybe, a grizzly takes time out to stretch while munching berries on Sable Pass just as the clouds part to reveal the awesome bulk of Mount McKinley for one magic moment.

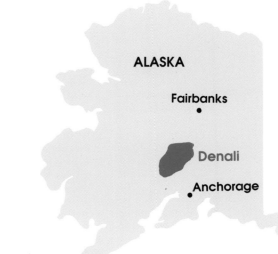

ALASKA

Fairbanks

Denali

Anchorage

Mount McKinley

Already the tallest mountain in North America, Mount McKinley rises a little higher each year above the tundra-covered valleys of Denali National Park. The mountain sits atop a major geologic feature called the Denali fault, where two of the giant plates that make up the earth's crust are colliding. The Alaska Range along with Mount McKinley is on the northern plate, which geologists believe is overriding the southern plate. As the two plates continue on their courses, the landmass below the mountain is pushed down as Mount McKinley itself is pushed up.

Mount McKinley has attracted mountain climbers to trudge up its slopes since 1897, when it was announced that "America's rival to Everest" had been discovered. After a climb to the lower north summit in 1909 by four miners nicknamed the "Sourdoughs," the true south summit was successfully attained by four Alaskans, one of them a native, in 1913. Today climbers usually try for the top in May or early June since after that avalanches threaten. Most climbers take a ski plane to the 7,500 level of the Kahiltna Glacier to begin the 10 to 20 day trek.

Denali National Park

Established:	1917
Location:	Alaska
When to go:	Open all year. (Late-May to mid-September is the main season.)
Size:	6,028,091 acres
Wildlife:	Grizzly bear, moose, caribou, Dall sheep, wolf, fox, golden eagle, loon, wolverine, marmot, pika, small mammals, and birds
Terrain:	Mountains, tundra, valleys, and lakes
Interesting sights:	Mount McKinley and Wickersham Wall
Activities:	Ranger-led walks, hikes, children's programs, sled-dog demonstrations, slide shows, and films; bus tours, hiking, fishing, rafting, cross-country skiing, mountain climbing, and backpacking
Services:	Three visitor centers, three lodges, cabins, and seven campgrounds
Information:	P.O. Box 9, Denali National Park, Alaska 99755; 907-683-2294

In a world dominated by white snow and black granite, the subtle color variations of Polychrome Pass seem much more startling than they would in a less stark environment.

Index